The Pursuit of Freedom

The Pursuit of Freedom
Four Steps to a Lifestyle of Walking in Freedom

Tassyane Assis

THE PURSUIT OF FREEDOM
Copyright © 2023 by Tassyane Assis
All rights reserved. This book is protected by the copyright laws of United States of America. No part of this book may be reproduced, distributed, or transmitted in any form or by any means, including photocopying, recording, or other electronic or mechanical methods, without the prior written permission of the publisher. Permission will be granted upon request.

Published in Miami, Florida by New Life Publishing House.

New Life Publishing House titles may be purchased in bulk for educational, business, fund raising or promotional purposes. For more information, please email admin@newlifepublishinghouse.life.

Disclaimer: The names and details surrounding the stories have been changed to protect the identity of individuals. Any association with specific individuals is purely unintended.

Disclaimer: This book is not therapy. This book is only for informational and educational purposes and should not be considered therapy or any form of treatment. We are not able to respond to specific questions or comments about personal situations, appropriate diagnosis, or treatment, or otherwise provide any clinical opinions.

The Freedom Technique was created by Michelle Goncalves. For more information on the technique, please contact Michelle at Mjjkag@me.com.

Scripture quotations are from:
The Amplified Bible (AMP)
© 1965, 1987 by Zondervan Publishing House.
The Amplified New Testament © 1958, 1987 by the Lockman Foundation.

The Message (MSG)
© 1993, 1994, 1995, 1996, 2000, 2001, 2002
Used by permission of NavPress Publishing Group

The Passion Translation® (TPT)
copyright © 2017 by BroadStreet Publishing Group, LLC.
Used by permission. All rights reserved.

The Holy Bible, New International Version (NIV)
© 1973, 1978, 1984, 2011 by Biblica, Inc.™
Used by permission. All rights reserved worldwide.

The Holy Bible, King James Version (KJV)

Holy Bible, New Living Translation (NLT)
© 1996, 2004 by Tyndale Charitable Trust.
Used by permission of Tyndale House Publishers.
All rights reserved.

NEW LIFE PUBLISHING HOUSE LLC. Miami, Florida.
https://newlifepublishinghouse.life

Cover Art by: Louise Lobo
Cover Design by: Antonio Guerra
Interior Design by: Mia with LKJ Books
Editors: Thomas Womack, Path To Publishing Editing Team

ISBN HC: 978-1-961787-01-8
ISBN Paperback: 978-1-961787-00-1
ISBN eBook: 978-1-961787-02-5

Library of Congress Cataloging-in-Publication Data

Name: Assis, Tassyane, author.
Publisher: New Life Publishing House, LLC.
Title: The Pursuit of Freedom - Four Steps to a Lifestyle of Walking in Freedom
Identifier: LCCN 2023915740 | ISBN 978-1-961787-00-1 (Paperback)

Printed in United States of America

10 9 8 7 6 5 4 3 2 1

To YOU,
a believer in Jesus Christ,
freedom fighter,
and freedom seeker.

Contents

Acknowledgments..1
Preface..4
Introduction..9
Step I: Understanding Freedom..11
   1. A Glimpse into My Own Pursuit of Freedom..13
   2. What Does the World Say Freedom Is?..21
   3. What Does the Bible Say Freedom Is?..26
   4. How the Subconscious Plays a Role in Our Freedom..........................42
Step II: Pursuing Freedom from a Place of Victory..49
   5. Because We Are Victorious, We Can! So…How, What, and When?....51
   6. Because We Are Victorious, We Are Free to Love..................................64
   7. Who Wants to Keep the Victorious Ones from Freedom?...................74
   8. Because We Are Victorious, There Is Grace for the Journey................86
Step III: Pursuing Freedom from a Place of Identity.....................................93
   9. You Are Free of a Sinful Nature..97
   10. You Are Free to Be Salt and Light..105
   11. You Are Free to Be You— And Not Compare Yourself....................111
   12. You Are Free to Multiply...116
Closing Comments on the Pursuit of Freedom..120
Step IV: Freedom Technique..123
   13. Introduction to the Freedom Technique and Its Founder...............125
   14. What Is the Freedom Technique?..127
   15. Freedom Technique in Action..129
   16. Real-Life Examples...136
Credits—Freedom Technique..141
Bonus: Empowering Identity Declarations...142
Bonus: More Empowering Scriptures on Biblical Freedom......................145
About the Author...151

Acknowledgments

First and foremost, all honor and glory to God. It is only through Him that we can grow and pursue freedom, and only by His grace is it even possible.

Many people in my life have helped me in my freedom journey. They've influenced my belief system, and they've also influenced how freedom is defined in my life. I've learned from their daily conversations, from their messages I hear, and from their books that I read. It's impossible to mention and honor every name without doing someone the injustice of leaving them out. If you have ever done life with me, I owe you some credit for who I am.

As much as I want to list all the names in the world and give everyone proper credit, I don't know how I can do that. But here are a few names of those who have significantly contributed to this project.

At the beginning of my Christian walk, Thiago Teixeira was my first mentor. He spent countless hours teaching me and building a solid foundation for everything I now know. He's one of the freest people that I have met. When faced with a biblical conflict, he inquires from God what the scripture means instead of assuming he knows it all. He does that in humility while sticking to the truth of the Word of God. I haven't met anyone who knows Scripture as well as he does. He taught me to do the same. He taught me how to study the Bible, and who I am according to its truth. I'm forever indebted and grateful to him.

My husband, Omar Gonzalez, is a man after God's own heart. He truly exemplifies a husband loving his wife like Christ loves the church, allowing her to make her own mistakes and learn from them while keeping her within his protective gaze so she won't be lost when she realizes she made too many mistakes. He is my favorite human, the love of my life.

Our three girls, Meyre, Ayane, and Daniela, encourage me and challenge me to discover new levels of freedom as a mother and human. They've been one of God's top channels to lead me to discover that more freedom is always available. They are incredible.

My mother, an extraordinary woman, has prayed for me without ceasing since always. Her prayers have kept me alive, and I aspire to be like her in many ways.

My father in many ways has shaped me and pushed me in further levels of freedom by simply being who he is—my earthly father, with the heart of my heavenly Father.

My sister, Poincyane Assis-Nascimento, is one of my favorite human beings, my best friend forever and divine association. Words can't describe my love for her.

My beautiful friends who make up our Support System Group—Mislene Bonetti, Telma Muniz, and my sister, of course—are my go-to ladies. Through our talking and sharing, we grow and heal and expand our capacity to understand more and better what God is doing in our lives. I cannot thank Him enough for giving me such extraordinary ladies to do life with. I love them deeply.

My friend Michelle Gonçalves, through her technique to reach personal freedom, has inspired me to write this book. Without a doubt, my conversation with her about her technique was the birth of this book in the Spirit. She was extremely generous to share her technique with all of us through this book. She holds a special place in my heart, and I love her.

My friend Lori Hogg has shared a beautiful testimony that illustrated one of the important points of this book so well. I love her wholeheartedly. Our conversations are always deep and always filled with divine revelation, making us both better people.

My brother, Bruno Alexsander, and my sister-in-law, Daniela Assis, do such a beautiful job raising up their children in freedom, while showing them the right path, away from the fear of man. My brother has a heart after the Father's heart, as my husband and my father do, and it's beautiful to watch their pursuit of freedom as they do life together.

My brother-in-law, Junior Nascimento (I couldn't leave him

out!), is someone I met back when we were teenagers. Seeing the change in him because of his relationship with Jesus brings a smile to my face any time of day!

Vicki introduced me to silent retreats. These retreats had been in the heart of God for me from the moment I said yes to Jesus as an adult, and I knew it. She was the person God used to make it a reality in my life. Since my first experience in silence back in 2018, I've made it a habit to get away with Jesus as often as possible. She has played an important role in this for me, in an important season of my life.

Pastor Caleb was present at the Colorado retreat in August 2019 when I first penciled this book. He encouraged everyone to spend time in scriptures from the book of Romans that were the backbone of this book.

Pastor Fabio Nascimento, my pastor, led me to Christ years ago and is one of my great encouragers. He constantly reminds me of God's anointing over my life. He is amazing, and I'm grateful for his leadership and spiritual covering. He carries such peace, love, and wisdom, and I appreciate these things about him.

Gisah Batista Janzen, who I met after I penned the original words of this book, has been essential to my continuous personal pursuit of freedom. And her husband, Konrad Janzen, gave me the simplest yet one of the most relevant words during probably the hardest time I've experienced in my life thus far.

Tiffany and Fernanda, who read the book, most definitely helped me make some corrections and gave me some valuable feedback and insights before it made to my wonderful editor, Thomas.

Thank you all.

Preface

Have you ever gotten a phone call to join a friend for coffee, and that casual coffee ends up being a life-changing moment?

It was an ordinary day when I was going about my normal house chores and busy life. A friend of mine called and invited me to have coffee with her. She said she wanted to introduce me to a daily meditation technique she'd created and developed for herself. She said she named it The Freedom Technique, and that she'd been using it daily during her prayer time. She went on to tell me how amazing and liberating it had been for her in the past few months.

I sat in my dining room, listening to her, but at the same time, not listening to her at all because the Holy Spirit began speaking to me. I understood there was more to this invitation than just coffee. I understood that this was a divine invitation to partner with heaven for something greater. My mind could not yet comprehend what it was, but my spirit did, and it was screaming, *Yes, yes, and yes!*

Has that ever happened to you? You know something great is happening, and you're excited, but you can't really fully understand why. I believe this happens when our spirits are capturing something that our minds can't wrap themselves around just yet, but it's good. And only God knows how long it may be before our minds catch up. For me, in this case, it has been almost four years! And that's okay.

When my friend called about having coffee, she wanted me to help her adapt this technique to a level that anyone could relate to, even nonbelievers. She knew this technique could help many, regardless of their age, faith, religious background, or level of spirituality. She knew this technique could help people encounter and experience the truth—and the truth will set you *free*! Hence the name Freedom Technique.

I agreed. I was up for the challenge. In fact, I didn't feel like I had a choice, because my spirit jumped with a yes before I could even think of anything else. Of course, we all know we have a choice, but that was my spirit's default choice. I'm passionate about helping others find freedom. However, to be completely honest, I felt unequipped and inadequate for the task. But if there's one thing I've learned—and I know we've all heard this, but I continue to learn to live and walk in these words daily—God doesn't call the equipped, He equips the called. And He has called me to restore the saints, which is the passion and the impulse of my heart. So yes, my answer was a burning and absolute yes.

When we sat down for coffee together, I took lots of notes as she explained in more detail to me what she'd created. I did my best to capture her heart as she spoke so passionately about the freedom she had sought for so long and had finally begun to achieve, in so many areas of her life. I saw the joy on her face, the radiant look in her eyes, and finally, a new level of freedom beaming out of her spirit like I'd never seen before. My spirit rejoiced as it captured the power of what was happening in the spirit realm.

Afterward, I went back home and immediately positioned myself to work on the notes I'd taken with my friend. I presented it all to God and asked Him to lead the way, and as I did that, I had a vision. It was a book, and I saw the word *Freedom*. Before I even touched any notes, God began to show me that this book was beyond my friend's technique. It was a book He was giving me to write. It was born from our meeting, but it was beyond that. The vision proceeded to show how this book would lead many souls into freedom. I saw the Spirit of God alive, moving through the book as people read it, stirring them up inside as they learn to walk in His freedom—the freedom He paid such a high price for each of us to have. I saw a multitude of people and nations weeping, as prison doors were being opened in the Spirit. I saw chains being broken supernaturally, as people chose to believe that what God said is true, and that in fact He is enough.

I was in awe. And again, I couldn't fully understand what I was experiencing or why, but I knew my spirit got it, so I simply came into agreement with it and said yes. I still felt ill-equipped to do the task at hand, but I was excited nonetheless. And I said, "Yes, Lord, let's do it. I have no idea what and how, but let's do it!"

I was then led to look up the word freedom in the dictionary and take notes of what it meant. And then to research the word freedom in the Bible. Simple but complete research, just taking notes on it. As the Spirit led me, I did this. I took a brand-new notebook, wrote the word "Freedom" on it, and took notes of my findings.

That's when I began to realize how crooked our definition of freedom is. And I heard God in my spirit as He asked me this question: How can people be free if they don't even know what freedom is?

As if I wasn't overwhelmed enough with all I just described, God proceeded to tell me that I would be writing this book in Colorado—just a couple months later—in a silent retreat I planned to attend.

Later, as I was packing to go to Colorado, God reminded me to bring the "Freedom" notebook I'd started, plus a few different Bible translations, since we wouldn't have access to electronics or the internet during the retreat. He reminded me that we would be writing this book in the next couple of days. I packed everything I felt like He was leading me to pack—though I must admit I wasn't taking the writing part too seriously.

I got to Colorado, and on the first morning there, I was quietly having my coffee when this dialogue began in my spirit:
— Ready? (God asks me.)
— Ready for what?
— To write the book!
— Oh! So, You were serious!?
— Of course.
— I can't write a book like that. I have nothing to type on, no internet to research with.
— You are right, daughter. You cannot. But I can. And I am inviting you to do it with Me. Are you ready?
— Yes. (Again, the only answer I wanted to give Him.)

I took the notebook where I'd begun writing my research on freedom, I took all my Bibles and a couple of pens, and I went to sit outside, looking at the beautiful mountains I never get to see in South Florida. And that's how this book was initially written. In eight hours, the book was written from beginning to end. He even gave me a picture of the cover in a vision and showed me the person who was to draw it. By the end, I'd moved inside to the dining room table. When I penned the last word, I broke out into what I don't even know it was—it was laughter, crying, tears, a mixture of tremendous joy, accomplishment, and gratitude at its finest. I don't even have words to describe what I felt at that moment. I'd never experienced a moment like that, and I haven't experienced it again since.

Yes, of course, I had penned all those words. I felt my hand about to fall off from it all. But I didn't come up with the words. It was as if the Holy Spirit whispered them to me as I wrote them down.

And then, for the next four years, I believe it was a mixture of living out those words and translating them alongside the Holy Spirt in a way that makes sense to others. The words unfolded and came off the paper into the computer onto the actual pages of the book you're now holding. These past four years have been intense for me; I had to fight and pursue my personal freedom with all my might.

I titled the book *The Pursuit of Freedom* because freedom is something we're constantly pursuing by seeking the face of the Freedom Giver. It's not something we find once and never have to look for again. It is ever growing, ever changing, ever fascinating.

The pursuit of freedom has become a way of life for me. I hope it does for you too.

It's true that Jesus has already died to set us *free*—this is already done—but *we* are not done. We're still here, living in a broken and fallen world, growing daily from glory to glory and freedom to freedom. We have received the gift of freedom, full freedom, and now we pursue it to learn how to live in it fully.

The words you will read in this book are my best attempt to partner with the Holy Spirit to translate the heart of God for the freedom He desires you to have in every area of your life.

It's important that you know I'm not into that new-agey, enlighten-yourself-and-become-better-every-day type of teachings. I believe there's a fine line between that and the truth of what the pure gospel offers us. And that line is drawn by Jesus. While I'm attempting to bring attention to what is our responsibility as humans to do for ourselves to grow and improve and become better, we must know that we can do it only because of His grace that has made a way for us. It's not by our own power, but by the power of the Holy Spirit in us.

Being free seems like something so simple. And it is. But simple does not equal easy. As a matter of fact, many may think they're free. We usually associate freedom with not being in prison or maybe living in a country where we have freedom of speech. The reality is that freedom is something much deeper, much more profound, and way beyond what we may know and consider freedom to be. Being mentally and emotionally free has little to do with our physical freedom. Freedom is an internal condition, not an external condition. In fact, a person could be in chains and yet be free. And the opposite is also true. A person can have no physical restraint at all and yet be a slave. A slave to their own sins. A slave to a lifestyle. A slave to a mindset or thought pattern that keeps that person living below their fullest potential. A slave to emotional dependencies. A slave to a belief system that keeps the person blindfolded and therefore unable to see all the opportunities around them. A slave to a culture, customs, and traditions that may go against the truth of the Word of God. A slave to the fear of man, which translates into a constant need to please others and perform, no matter the cost, even in abusive situations. Bondage.

I'll ask you the same question I heard God asking me while I was doing the research: "How can we be free when we don't even know what freedom is?" How can we be something that we can barely describe what it is?

You probably have the answer right: We cannot.

This book is designed with one single purpose in mind: To bring you more freedom. Regardless of how free you think you are (or aren't), there is *more* freedom. There's always a next level. And the purpose of this book is to bring you to that next level of freedom, through a deepening of your relationship and intimacy with the Freedom Giver. In the Word of God, Jesus says that the truth will set you free (John 8:32). That is my prayer for *you*, who have chosen to pick up this book in search of freedom.

Love,
Tassyane

Introduction

While writing this book at the retreat, I had a clear vision of what the table of contents should look like. It was divided into parts, and those parts became "steps."

Step I is the research part, including an opening chapter in which I share just a glimpse of my personal pursuit from the past four years.

Step II is about pursuing freedom from a place of victory. We already have freedom; we aren't running after it. Within these chapters, we'll find details on how to pursue it from the right place, victorious in Christ.

Step III is pursuing freedom from a place of identity. It's imperative that we know who we are, and that we're pursuing freedom from our true identity.

And Step IV is the Freedom Technique that my friend created, and that I helped her put into words. I know you'll find it helpful and practical for daily use in your time with God as He leads you in your own pursuit of freedom.

I've included "activations" for you after each chapter of the first three steps, and I pray that you enjoy them. They'll help activate your spirit in each step that we take toward freedom.

And finally, I ask that you consider the vision God gave me for this book (as I shared in the preface), and the promises He has for the readers who would pick up this book at any point and time. Because if you believe it, you will receive it!

Step I

UNDERSTANDING FREEDOM

*"May we think of freedom not as the right to do as we please,
but as the opportunity to do what is right."*
Peter Marshall

In Step I, you'll read about my research of the word freedom, both from the dictionary as well as from the Bible. Even if you don't enjoy research, I believe you'll be enlightened. Defining what we're trying to achieve, pursue, and conquer is essential.

Two of the chapters in Step I are all about defining the word freedom. If you love definitions and you find yourself receiving even more revelations in these verses, you're one of my kind. Write it down, and make sure you capture every word that you believe the Holy Spirit is speaking to you. I know that He will be encountering you during this reading and bringing you into deep levels of freedom.

Before we get to the definitions, I'll share a glimpse of my personal pursuit of freedom over the past few years. It's definitely personal and vulnerable. I found myself in a place and time in my life when I realized I had to pursue a deeper level of His freedom with intention and intensity each and every day. It was a time when an ugly reality hit me, and I had to choose between pursuing the higher reality I knew I had access to or being stuck in a place I didn't want to be.

Finally, the last chapter of this step is on how the subconscious mind plays a role in our freedom.

One

A Glimpse into My Own Pursuit of Freedom

*"Peter spoke up and said,
'But Lord, where would we go?
No one but you gives us the revelation of eternal life.'"*
John 6:68 TPT, 2017

I recently heard a teaching from one of my favorite pastors on John 6:68, and what he said led me to a revelation from the Holy Spirit. I realized that Peter was having what I like to call a spirit-to-spirit freedom moment. That's when our spirit receives something from the Lord, and it comes alive from agreeing, but our mind cannot comprehend it yet. I have so many of those moments that I thought I was a little slow. But no, it turns out our spirit is outside of time, alongside the Spirit of God, who is sometimes light-years ahead of what our minds can perceive, because our mind is limited to time.

In the context of this verse, Jesus was preaching what seemed to be an awkwardly odd message about eating His flesh and drinking His blood. It didn't seem to be popular; everyone left—everyone except His disciples. And when He asked if they too would leave, Peter responded, "Where would we go? No one but you gives us the revelation of eternal life."

I don't believe the disciples understood the message any more than the people who left, but they stayed because their spirits came alive. They may not have comprehended with their intellect, but their spirits were in alignment. Their spirits were ahead of their minds, and their spirits were saying yes, although they had no idea to what. They just had a conviction that Jesus was the real deal, the only one who had the keys to eternal life.

I call this a spirit-to-spirit freedom moment. It's a moment when you give yourself permission to say yes before you understand with your mind. And when you do that, you give the Holy Spirit permission to bring you to the next level of freedom. I've had so many remarkable experiences and encounters with the Lord that led me to deeper levels of freedom, and they all came from these spirit-to-spirit freedom moments.

One of the major breakthroughs in my life was an experience that led to the restoration of my relationship with my father. I was thirty-two years old at the time, and I'd never had a smooth relationship with him. But one day, I decided I wanted to honor him. So I asked God how to do that, because I didn't know. I asked God to show me one good thing about my dad, and I would call him to tell him, without any expectation of him ruining my day.

God answered quickly. I called my father, and even during that phone call, I was able to see him from a completely different perspective. It was as if he was a completely different human being. Except that it wasn't him who had changed. It was me—my perspective, my vision, my ability to see my father from God's eyes, with God's eyes. I couldn't believe that I could actually see him that way. I could understand the reasons why he did everything he did throughout his whole life, as wrong as they could have been. Not that this made it right, but I saw him from God's eyes: forgiven, justified, righteous, holy. I felt no bitterness toward him, no resentment, no anger, no hurt. Just pure and unconditional love.

This experience was beyond me. My mind didn't fully comprehend how it just happened, but my spirit was in full agreement. It wasn't a fleeting change that went away when his human flaws came to the surface. No, that's how I see him still. It's who he is, period. And because of that, that's how I began to treat him from that day forward, and how I began to speak to him. And still do, to this day. This brought me to a new level of freedom in every single area of my life.

This experience with my father came from seeking God for freedom in a specific area. And it truly opened up so many more areas than I expected. Consequentially, it also unlocked something in me that I didn't know was possible. Suddenly, I began to see people differently. I realized I was seeing them through God's eyes instead of my own. That was major freedom for me.

Prior to that, I'd come to repentance for things I did that I previously didn't think were wrong, and it took me to places of freedom that I didn't think were possible. I had learned to renew my mind about the way I approach my ideas to people, about the way I share my heart and express my emotions. I had learned, for the most part, to communicate without anger. I had learned not to speak so quickly with my impulses but to wait and pray instead, and to speak only when my heart was at ease. (Although I must admit, that last one seemed to be a work in progress for years). I had many experiences that truly took me to deeper levels of freedom with the Lord. I was at a good place when He first gave me the concept of this book, and I thought I was living in full freedom. Little did I know I was about to get on a wild ride to learn to fight for and pursue a lifestyle of deeper freedom.

As life continued to happen, after the retreat, things began to shift. I experienced a couple of incidents, one with each of my daughters, that brought me to the realization that when faced with situations that were highly stressful and emotional, I was emotionally unavailable to be fully present for them, because guilt and shame took over all my senses, and I shut down. They'd come to me with a real problem, and instead of being the mother they needed me to be at that moment, I was subconsciously shifting the blame and my other feelings onto them, making them feel even worse than they did when the conversation began. I was miserable and filled with those negative emotions, and my girls were hurt and felt like they couldn't connect with their own mother.

Suddenly, I felt as though all the freedom I'd known was gone. I didn't understand how or why, much less what to do about it. If Jesus had already set me free, why was I dealing with such a lack of freedom? Why was I feeling like I was in bondage? What happened to all the freedom I had before?

Then I began to observe that besides those two major incidents, I did the same thing often, in various ways, with people I love the most. I couldn't handle what I thought was the emotional weight of carrying the blame for their hurt. This whole concept that was being brought up to my attention by God about shifting blame was foreign to me, because I'm pretty good at taking responsibility for things and owning up to them. But what happens when there's nothing to own up to?

I experienced a downward spiral for a couple of years before I hit rock bottom. However, I'm generally a positive person, in a good mood and laughing. I'm emotionally stable and put together for the most part. Nobody could tell I was in the middle of a crisis—nor could I, as a matter of fact. I was completely oblivious to it. Until one day, it hit me completely by surprise.

But it wasn't a surprise to God. He had been preparing me for this for years, even without my consciously knowing. God always prepares us for each crisis that comes our way.

One day, in what seemed to be a normal afternoon, I got a call from the emergency room saying my daughter was there. My heart dropped. I wanted to throw up. Meanwhile, on that same day, my other daughter was experiencing a whole set of issues. That was the day my whole world, as I knew it, fell apart. I began to have flashbacks of visions and dreams I'd had in the few months leading up to that, and I began to understand what God had been trying to show me. He had been preparing my heart for this day for months. I didn't understand, but my heart had been prepared nonetheless. For that, I was grateful—and at the same time, in so much pain that it was surreal. Both my daughters seemed to be so broken, going through so much pain, and there seemed to be absolutely nothing I could do about it.

Freedom, it seemed, had escaped me. But the truth is, freedom is progressive. The freedom we already walk in is the only reason we're able even to recognize certain things in our lives that can lead us to the next level. So before I continue with the story, I'll briefly tell you what got me through the pain and equipped me for the times I had ahead of me.

The next day, I received a call from a friend from Brazil who was in Miami at the time. She invited me for a night of worship. Who worships while in so much pain? Well, apparently, I do! My spirit jumped with a yes before I could consciously say no. I guess it was better than sitting home alone crying in my misery, although that's what I wanted to do. Quite frankly, deep inside, I think that's what I thought I deserved. After all, my kids were in pain, and in my mind, it was always my fault—so I had to be in pain too. But God doesn't give us what we deserve. He gives us His magnificent grace. I got ready, and I went.

That night was a divine gift to me. And that night equipped me with so much more than I can begin to comprehend, even today. That night, I believe God deposited in my spirit strength beyond my ability to wrap my mind around. It made no sense to me. Nothing made any sense at all. The things I saw in the spirit, the things I heard, the things spoken over me—the fire tunnel, and the angels, angels I'd never seen before, though I've read about them in the Bible, and I know their assignments. Nothing made any natural sense. But my spirit agreed with His, and that's all that mattered.

That night, someone said to me, "There is more freedom. Pursue His freedom." My mind did not get it. It seemed so simple, yet so profound and complex. But again, my spirit totally got it. And I said yes to it. As those words encountered my spirit, and as soon as I said yes to it, even without knowing what I was saying yes to, it was as if I'd received an instant deposit, a spiritual download. I understood how to fight for others' freedom at a new level, and I understood I needed to pursue my own freedom and how to do it. I understood that I hadn't *lost* my freedom. As a matter of fact, I was being invited to a new level of freedom. And I understood that this was my only choice. Unless, of course, I wanted to stay in misery, which I didn't.

Back to the story. The next few months were hard, very hard. But I was so strengthened by the Lord. I had powerful experiences with the Holy Spirit daily that got me through one day at a time. I understood this was a time of healing, in which the Lord was freeing me of some issues that were keeping me captive. I cleared my agenda, and each day, I sat as the Holy Spirit led, and I didn't do much more than pray and meditate on the Word of God. I went back to dreams I had and previous words He had spoken, and He started making sense of them and freeing my mind in unexpected ways.

I understood that I'm good at taking responsibility and ownership. The problem is that when there's nothing for me to take responsibility for, I subconsciously begin to look for blame. And if the blame isn't mine, I assume it must be someone else's. And that's not always the case. There doesn't have to be someone to blame or someone to take responsibility for every occurrence. Sometimes things just happen, and God will deal with the people who need to be dealt with at His time, and that's it. I just needed to be okay with that, and I wasn't. Subconsciously, I wanted to fix every situation. I wanted to control the outcome because I thought it would be safer for the people I love.

This revelation completely freed me from the blame-shifting I'd done subconsciously and involuntarily my entire life. That was huge!

I understood that it's not wrong to be positive and maybe even oblivious in the middle of a crisis, because the truth is that we live in a reality that's superior to the temporary reality of this earth—a reality in which there's no crisis. Having a hyper-awareness of the current reality may hinder our ability to remain in Him and His higher reality. The key is to keep our spirits aligned with His and our hearts prepared, because we don't know the future.

The only way we can possibly do that with our spirit and our heart is by daily surrendering our lives to Jesus and fully trusting that He has our best interest in mind. Living in daily, intimate, spirit-to-spirit relationship and freedom moments with Him, so when the time comes that it seems like our world as we know it falls apart, the default reaction of our spirits will be to worship and not collapse.

As I continued to pursue God and His freedom, He continued to reveal areas of my life where I needed freedom. The more freedom we have, the better we're able to identify the areas where we need more freedom, and the more natural the whole process becomes. I started to restore my relationship with my daughters. I was able to recognize my limitations of the past, to explain and apologize to them, to ask for their forgiveness, and to forgive myself. I began to earn their trust by showing compassion and kindness toward them, and loving them beyond my own ability to love. More than a motherly love, but Jesus's love loving through me.

All it took was my yes. My willingness to be vulnerable to God and intentional about pursuing my freedom and fighting for theirs. Even without fully understanding it at the time.

Throughout this process, God taught me that pursuing my freedom is allowing Him to show me the areas where I need freedom, and trusting His timing—while doing my part, which is to follow His lead. Because rapid growth isn't always healthy growth. I don't have to understand everything. I just have to trust the One who knows everything.

I also learned that fighting for the freedom of others—in this case, my children, but I believe it applies to anyone—isn't pointing out their flaws or trying to control the outcome. It is seeing them through His eyes, truly and solely, and calling that new reality into existence in the way that I treat them and speak to them on a daily basis. Simple? Yes! Easy? No. Because sometimes, the temporary reality tries to get in the way, and we must learn to stand our ground with God, trusting what He has spoken.

Experiencing His healing love in such amorous way over our lives and our home led me to a series of events that freed me from different limiting beliefs I never realized I had, or that I thought I'd already dealt with. Perhaps I had, but there was more—another layer.

I'm sharing all this with you to say that I've been seeking God and His freedom for many years, and just when I thought I was living in the fullness of it, He showed me there was more. In fact, there's always more. If we ever think we're done, as I did, we're only limiting ourselves from experiencing the more that He has for us.

This journey has been greatly intensified since I first penned this book, and I don't believe it was only for my sake but for yours as well. I encourage you to be like the disciples of Jesus when they heard teachings that perhaps they didn't comprehend, but their spirits came alive, and they said, "Yes, we will remain." I encourage you not to try to understand it all, but instead allow the Holy Spirit to lead you. He is so good at it!

In the same way that He'd been preparing me to pursue my freedom for such time as this—and continues to do so—I believe He has been preparing you to pursue your freedom for such as time as this! Testimonies carry a spirit of prophecy that invites the Holy Spirit to do it again. I believe He is wanting to set people free and restore areas in their lives where they may not even be aware that restoration is needed. He is wanting to bring them to a level of freedom they didn't realize was possible.

Perhaps it all starts with you and your personal pursuit of freedom. He has been preparing you for it. All He needs is your yes.

Activation

Our first activation is super simple. You'll receive an impartation from the Holy Spirit as you say yes to Him in your pursuit of freedom.

You'll read this simple scenario, then close your eyes and imagine the scenario playing out in your mind.

Don't worry that you're making it up. You probably aren't. The Holy Spirit is most likely leading you through it. Just go with it.

Afterward, take note of every detail and meditate on it with the Lord. Ask Him if there's anything else, and journal that as well.

Imagine you are sitting with Jesus.

He lays a hand on you to give you His vision, His courage, love, compassion, boldness.

He asks you: Do you want to embark on this lifelong journey with Me? A journey of pursuing and walking in pure freedom. The freedom I have already paid a price for you to have.

What is your answer to Him?

It doesn't have to be a yes if you don't feel ready. You can tell Him if you aren't feeling ready and why.

This is a safe space for you to be vulnerable, open, and honest with Jesus.

Until you are ready to give Him your yes.

Two

What Does the World Say Freedom Is?

"Most people do not really want freedom because freedom assumes responsibility, and most people are afraid of that."
Sigmund Freud

I knew a manager many years ago who believed wholeheartedly that he was totally free. He was a great leader, talented and gifted in many ways. I'll refer to him as Magnus. He led the organization fairly well, and in many ways, I could tell that he had a genuine desire to see people succeed. But there was one thing that really hindered his growth and freedom. Magnus was jealous of other people's talents. He believed freedom is the right to act, speak, or think as one wants without hindrance or restraint. He valued the quality of being frank, open, or outspoken, and freedom of expression. And he used all that to convince people to stay at a place that was better for them. Except that it wasn't better for them at all. It was better for *him,* because they made him feel threatened. He used what he called freedom in order to manipulate others.

Because he was a great leader, people believed him. But honestly, he was acting out of fear, insecurity, and jealousy—subconsciously, perhaps. I'm not sure. The fact is, he was a slave to that insecurity, fear, and jealousy, even if subconsciously. But freedom would mean assuming responsibility and admitting the jealousy, the insecurities, the feeling threatened. And that was scary. It was safer to be in control. But control isn't freedom at all.

Is there an area in your life where you feel you absolutely must stay in control? That may be a red flag, an indication that something behind your conscious mind may be worth digging into with the Holy Spirit.

Is there someone like Magnus around you? Perhaps this is someone with whom you need to draw some boundaries, or even cut off the relationship. And if that's not possible, as in the case with a boss, just bring awareness.

In this chapter, I'll share my research of the word freedom according to several dictionaries and other reference books. As we explore these definitions, you'll understand what the world thinks freedom is, and you'll think, *Yes, agreed, that's freedom.* Think again, my friend. Because as much as Magnus thinks he is free—and he may be in many ways—he's a slave to jealousy and insecurity in a way that not only keeps him from experiencing the fullness of what God has designed for him, but may compromise the ministry God entrusted in his hands.

What is freedom, according to English-language dictionaries?

- Freedom is the power or right to act, speak, or think as one wants without hindrance or restraint.
- Freedom is the state of not being imprisoned or enslaved.
- Freedom is the absence of subjection to foreign domination or despotic government.
- Freedom is the state of being physically unrestricted and able to move easily.
- Freedom is the unrestricted use of something.
- Freedom is the power of self-determination attributed to the will, the quality of being independent of fate or necessity.

Example of freedom being used as a noun: *The prisoners made a desperate bid for freedom.*

Synonyms: liberty, liberation, release, emancipation, deliverance, delivery, discharge, nonconfinement, extrication.

Antonym: captivity.

Another example of freedom being used as a noun: *A national*

revolution was the only path to freedom.
Synonyms: independence, self-government, self-determination, self-legislation, self rule, home rule, sovereignty, autonomy, autarky, democracy, self-sufficiency, individualism, separation, nonalignment, emancipation, enfranchisement.
Antonym: dependence.

Another example: *They want freedom from local political accountability.*
Synonyms: exemption, immunity, dispensation, exception, exclusion, release, relief, reprieve, absolution, exoneration, impunity.
Antonyms: liability.

Another: *The law interfered with their freedom of expression.*
Synonyms: right to, entitlement to privilege, prerogative.

Another: *Patients have more freedom to choose who treats them.*
Synonyms: scope, latitude, leeway, margin, flexibility, facility, space, breathing space, room, elbow room, license, leave, free rein, a free hand, leisure, carte blanche.
Antonyms: restriction.

Another: *I admire her freedom of manner.*
Synonyms: naturalness, openness, lack of inhibition, lack of reserve, casualness, informality, lack of ceremony, spontaneity, ingenuousness.

Another: *He treats her with too much freedom.*
Synonyms: impudence, familiarity, overfamiliarity, presumption, forwardness.

More definitions:

- Freedom is the quality or state of being free: such as the absence of necessity, coercion, or constraint in choice or action, liberation from slavery or restraint or from the power of another: independence.
- Freedom is the quality or state of being exempt or released usually from something onerous; freedom from care.
- Freedom is the quality of being frank, open, or outspoken.
- Freedom is improper familiarity.
- Freedom is boldness of conception or execution.

And still more:

- Freedom is the condition or right of being able or allowed to do, say, think, etc., whatever you want to, without being controlled or limited.
- Freedom is the right to act in the way you think you should.
- Freedoms are rights given by the Constitution and the Bill of Rights, such as the freedom of speech, the right to say and write what you believe or think (with some limitations), and freedom of religion, the right to worship or to take part in religion.

When reading these definitions, what are your thoughts? For some of us, a couple of these can be alarming, but for the most part, we look at most of them and say, yes, it sounds about right. Our brain is trained to think this way. We've been living in a country—in a world, really—where these definitions are part of our culture, and our brains are trained to recognize these definitions as correct.

But what if I told you that some of them literally contradict what freedom is, according to the Bible? That's alarming, because it causes a battle in our minds between right and wrong. The Bible is the ultimate truth, unless we want to spend our entire lives in a freedom that, in reality, is not freedom at all.

I'll leave you with your own freedom to interpret as you will and to identify the differences for yourself. We've seen how the world defines freedom, which seems common and familiar, and right after our activation, we'll see how the Bible defines freedom. Enjoy it.

Activation

Let's take a moment now and ask the Holy Spirit to bring to our minds if there's anything we need to be aware of at this point.

Close your eyes and imagine Jesus next to you, taking away any anxieties and leading you to calm waters. Just breathe and stay there with Him for a moment.

Ask Him if there are any red flags He wants you to be aware of. Was there any particular point of the freedom research according to the world that you had a hard time letting go of?

What is He speaking to your heart?

Take notes of anything and everything you believe He is saying to you, even if you don't fully understand it yet.

Three

What Does the Bible Say Freedom Is?

*"True freedom is to be found only
when one escapes from oneself
and enters into the liberty of the children of God."*
François Fénelon

Before I became a believer, I really believed I had it all figured out. I had a deep conviction and passion for what I thought was right, and I wasn't afraid to stand up for myself, to boldly speak my mind, and to fight whoever I needed to fight. That, I believed, was freedom. I'd been that way since I was a kid, and honestly, it got me in trouble more times than I care to admit.

The truth is that these are good character traits deep inside, but I was so full of myself and arrogant. I was a slave to my own sense of righteousness and justice.

Once I became a believer, one of the gifts I received was the understanding of my identity as a child of God and the acceptance of His paternity, and so much that comes with it. Miraculously, I was able to look at myself as one looks at another person, to analyze what I was doing. I was able to escape myself, at least to some extent, and enter the liberty of the children of God. I could see that my righteousness was so crooked and partial, and completely erroneous at times. *My* justice—not just at all.

And I exchanged all that for *His* righteousness and justice.

The problem is that some believers still hold on to themselves, to their concepts, beliefs, and ideas. They fear that if they let go, there's nothing else.

The idea of this chapter is to let go of ourselves—of our concept of freedom, of our own understanding—and acknowledge God and His ways, allowing Him to do a work in us. I believe this is an invitation for all of us to let go and let God. Let God replace the concepts and beliefs that need to be replaced.

In this chapter, I'll introduce you to the biblical research I did on the word *freedom*. The Bible translations I used were *The Amplified Bible* and *The Message*. In each of the verses I'm introducing below, I found the word freedom, and therefore an implied definition for it, and I'm sharing those verses with you, along with the definition of freedom from each one and a brief elaboration according to my understanding of each verse in this context (freedom). I also used *The Passion Translation* for comments, further understanding, and research.

The Word of God is alive, and the same verse and the same passage can be looked at under many different lights. We're looking at these verses particularly to define freedom. Please don't confuse it with extracting single verses from Scripture to prove a point. Hermeneutics is the art of allowing the Bible to explain and interpret itself, and we're doing that here. It's a word-search method of Bible study using hermeneutic skills to find the definition of a particular word within the Bible itself without any other resource. We aren't using verses out of context; we're simply looking at them to define freedom within the Bible. And again, I'm sharing my interpretation, which I believe in, having been inspired by the Holy Spirit in me. You have the right to look at it from a different point of view.

Let's get started.

> "This [deceptive] persuasion is not from Him who called you [to freedom in Christ]." (Galatians 5:8 AMP)

Freedom is the absence of deception. Freedom and deception cannot coexist, because deception is an enslaving factor that keeps people in a mindset that's not derived from God. The person who's deceived does not know that he or she is deceived, which makes that deception involuntary. Therefore, that person is a slave to deception.

I love how this passage reads in *The Passion Translation, 2017*:

> "The One who enfolded you into His grace is not behind this false teaching that you've embraced. Not at all! Don't you know that when you allow even a little lie into your heart, it can permeate your entire belief system?" (Galatians 5:8-9)

One little white lie that goes unnoticed can permeate our entire belief system and corrupt it all. And that is serious, because not only do we not know we're deceived when we're deceived, but sometimes we deceive others with no harmful intentions.

One day, I was sitting at a table with a couple of friends and their adult daughter. She made a comment about how traumatized she was about Santa Claus. She went on to share the story of how her parents made such an effort to make her believe Santa was real. They drank the milk, left cookie crumbs around, and spilled the milk a little. As she described the entire scene, my mind spun.

Of course, her parents thought it was cute. They had no ill intention, no malice whatsoever in their hearts, but she was deceived. She was led to believe a lie. And when she discovered the truth, she was devastated. How could her parents—the people she was supposed to trust—have lied to her in that manner?

Later, without mentioning any names, I was having this conversation with my eldest daughter, who was in her second year of psychology at the time. She and I were calculating the damage of the trauma that such inoffensive deception can cause in the belief system of a growing human being. That child could potentially be afraid of trusting others. Subconsciously, she may think everyone is bound to lie to her, and that at some point, everyone will. Or that child could potentially be afraid of vulnerability. If she was made fun of when she found out that what she believed wasn't true, and the people who were supposed to love and protect her had lied to her, now she would close off and be afraid ever to be vulnerable again. And of course, there is no intimacy without vulnerability.

Can you see how deep this little but not-so-little white lie can go?

I don't know if this was the case with my friend's daughter; I didn't go this far whatsoever in the conversation. But these are possibilities of how a little lie can permeate an entire belief system, and suddenly, we have a young adult who's a slave to a belief system unintentionally created by her own parents, who love her very much but just didn't know better. She isn't free to trust, and she isn't free to be vulnerable.

Can you see why and how freedom is the absolute absence of deception and lies? And can you see how hard this can be in the world we live in, when lies and deception are planted in us unintentionally, many times by people who love us the most?

This is why we're here, pursuing freedom—because there's always something more to be unveiled to us. This is why I ask you to be open and allow the Holy Spirit to work and do what He wills, even if you don't fully get it. When we're deceived, we don't know that we're deceived. If we did know, we would do something about it, right?

> "For you, my brothers were called to freedom; only do not let your freedom become an opportunity for the sinful nature (worldliness, selfishness), but through love serve and seek the best for one another." (Galatians 5:13 AMP)

Freedom is to be able to embrace our Christlike nature fully and to understand that sin is not our nature when we have Jesus. Freedom is to love and serve one another through love.

Believing you are something you are not, and not knowing your identity, is a form of deception. It's an enslaving factor that keeps us from experiencing true freedom. Love is the opposite of fear, which is the largest enslaving entity. Therefore, love will always lead to freedom.

Freedom is being able to do whatever we want, and yet wanting and choosing to do the right things—not only for ourselves, but for everyone around us—out of love. We choose this because we want to, and because we can, because we're empowered by love, and because we're free to do so.

Again, I love how *The Passion Translation* expresses this verse—it says so much, so beautifully!

> "Beloved ones, God has called us to live a life of freedom in the Holy Spirit. But don't view this wonderful freedom as an opportunity to set up a base of operations in the natural realm."

Freedom means that we become so completely free of self-indulgence that we become servants of one another, expressing love in all we do.

Freedom comes from being a child of God:

> "...the creation itself will also be freed from its bondage to decay [and gain entrance] into the glorious freedom of the children of God." (Romans 8:21 AMP)

God has already accepted us, adopted us, and made us all His children through Jesus. We just need to receive it and accept it.

Freedom is knowing how to receive, without having to perform, and without the need to give something in return. When we feel that every time we receive something, we owe something in return, that's the mentality of transaction, the mentality of the earthly realm. Everything on earth is a transaction. If I give you something, I must want something in return, right? Wrong. At least, that's not how it works with God, because He is not working from an earthly mentality, and He doesn't operate from a transaction standpoint. "For God so loved the world that he gave his one and only Son, that whoever believes in him shall not perish but have eternal life" (John 3:16 NIV). That's it. That passage doesn't go on to say we must now pay Him back by doing a list of chores! He simply gave because He loves.

Learning to receive and to operate outside of the transaction mentality is freedom. We must learn to receive, and learn to give.

> "Therefore, do not let what is a good thing for you [because of your freedom to choose] be spoken of as evil [by someone else]." (Romans 14:16 AMP)

> "Live as free people, but do not use your freedom as a cover or pretext for evil, but [use it and live] as bondservants of God." (1 Peter 2:16 AMP)

Freedom is knowing what is good in the eyes of God, and choosing it. Everything that comes from God is good. Knowing that, and choosing it, is freedom.

Knowing good from evil is necessary, because although we have the knowledge of good and evil, it's important to know *God's* good and to choose it. Not everything that seems good is from God. And not everything that is good in itself will always be the best choice for us. Freedom is making the right choices according to God's goodness. And some things that are part of God's goodness for us may be perceived as bad by the world, and sometimes even by people close to us.

A silly example that will quickly illustrate this for you. Imagine you have a six-year-old little boy. He may think ice cream for breakfast every day is good. Ice cream, in fact, is good. It tastes good. But you, as his parent, know that a good choice for his daily breakfast would be eggs, fruit, and oatmeal. You raise him up and teach him these choices.

A few years go by too quickly, and before you know it, you have a young adult who has moved away to college. That young adult is free to make his own breakfast choices now. If he is choosing ice cream every day, I'm afraid to say that young man is not free. He's either addicted to sugar, in bondage to a mindset of do-whatever-I-want-because-nobody-tells-me-what-to-do, or simply careless about his health altogether. None of this is freedom. He has a choice, and he knows what is good for him, but he's choosing what he knows is not good.

Technically we're free to do whatever we want, but not everything is good for us, and doing things that aren't good for us, just because we can, will ultimately lead to bondage in one way or another. Being free to do whatever we want and making the right choices is real freedom.

God puts boundaries in place for His children not to restrict us, but to protect us from what's outside those boundaries. Sometimes, we don't have a full picture of good and evil. We have only a taste of it, like the little boy with the ice cream. God's boundaries protect us because He sees the full picture.

> "Now the Lord is the Spirit, and where the Spirit of the Lord is, there is liberty [emancipation from bondage, true freedom]." (2 Corinthians 3:17 AMP)

Freedom is to be filled with the Spirit of God. To be filled with the Holy Spirit is to allow the Holy Spirit to reign in every area of our lives.

There's a difference between allowing the Holy Spirit to reign—making Him the Lord of each area of our lives—and simply inviting Him to be a part of it. I believe we often simply invite Jesus into our lives and ask Him to collaborate with us. We do everything we want, plan our own ways, and ask Him to bless it. But what He desires is for us to allow Him room to reign as King, as Lord in every area of our lives, and for us to collaborate with Him and follow His lead.

That is freedom—not having to be in control, but instead giving Him the space to reign.

> "Save others, snatching them out of the fire; and on some have mercy but with fear, loathing even the clothing spotted and polluted by their shameless immoral freedom." (Jude 23 AMP)

Freedom is understanding and knowing that what the world calls freedom may be bondage and an abomination to God.

Many times, we're tied up in our own beliefs of what we may think something is—freedom, in this case—and the beliefs from the world may hold us back from fully understanding the true meaning of it. If the Bible says that people are polluted by shameless and immoral freedom, it means that some people, even in those days, already had the wrong concept of freedom.

As King Solomon said long ago, there's nothing new under the sun. If people had such a wicked and corrupt idea of what freedom was all those many centuries ago, is there a possibility that you and I—or even worse, our children—may have a distorted idea of freedom as well? And is there a possibility that because we have a distorted idea, we're seeking and living the wrong freedom, and it's actually leading us into bondage that we may not even be aware of? Perhaps.

> "Were you a slave when you were called? Do not worry about that [since your status as a believer is equal to that of a free-born believer]; but if you are able to gain your freedom, do that." (1 Corinthians 7:21 AMP)

Freedom is a state of mind. We underestimate the importance of evaluating what we think about, and we therefore allow our minds to run wild, doing little to bring it under control. But the reality for believers in Christ is that our spirit, powered by the Holy Spirit, is in control of our mind. That is freedom.

> "And by conscience, I mean for the sake of the other man's, not yours. For why is my freedom [of choice] judged by another's conscience [another's ethics—another's sense of right and wrong]?" (1 Corinthians 10:29 AMP)

Freedom is understanding what is right in God's eyes and choosing to do that—not judging others on whether they choose the same or not, or whether they have the same understanding and revelation. A conviction can come only from the Holy Spirit. Everything we do must be from that conviction—that is freedom. We act out of conviction, never out of "I have to" or "religious duty."

Freedom is taking responsibility for our actions.

Freedom is taking ownership of our own lives and perspectives, constantly submitting them to God.

If humans only knew how much freedom there is in taking ownership and responsibility! Imagine living a life where other people's actions and reactions never affect your own mood, attitude, or decisions. Well, that's ultimately what happens when we take responsibility and ownership over our lives. We move and act and make decisions out of conviction, not out of performance or religious duty. We act and speak according to the impulses of the Holy Spirit, not according to our own impulses, and we don't worry at all about anything outside our control. That is full ownership of our own lives and not of other people's lives, which we have no control over. That is living in full conviction.

That is freedom. Our actions, reactions, attitudes, moods, and results depend on us and us alone. And yes, it's possible to live this way. It's a choice, followed by consistent actions toward that choice. Is it easy? Absolutely not! It's much easier to live under the complete delusion that we can control other people and outcomes by how brilliant we are. It's harder to actually exercise the self-control we have inside us. After all, that self-control is just a seed. There's a lot of time and effort involved before it fully grows and becomes a mature tree that produces a harvest of fruit.

> "For this perishable [part of us] must put on the imperishable [nature], and this mortal [part of us that is capable of dying] must put on immortality [which is freedom from death]." (1 Corinthians 15:53 AMP)

Freedom is to understand our nature in Christ.

When we accept Jesus as our Lord and Savior, the Bible says we're given a new nature; we're made new, and we're a new creation. Our new nature is Christ's nature, and it is free from eternal death. God has already done this for us. Our part is to believe and accept it, and to learn each day how to live in the freedom that He already died for us to have.

> "Christ purchased our freedom and redeemed us from the curse of the Law and its condemnation by becoming a curse for us—for it is written, 'Cursed is everyone who hangs [crucified] on a tree [cross].'" (Galatians 3:13 AMP)

Freedom is to fully understand and embrace what Jesus did for us on that cross, and to accept that the price for our freedom has already been paid. There's no need to work to pay a debt that has already been paid.

Imagine that you inherit a large home from the passing of a relative. The deed is at the bank. The home is completely paid for, and nothing is owed on it. But somehow, you've missed that part. You know you inherited this spacious home, and you moved in, but you continue making the regular mortgage payments you used to make on your two-bedroom cottage. You are so happy! Because you now have a six-bedroom home that you've inherited, and you continue making the payments on a simple two-bedroom place. I agree that would be great. Except that, it's even better. You don't have to make the payments at all! Because it's paid for. There are no payments to be made, not even what you used to make for your former house. You owe nothing. Zero. And the banker is so confused. He's waiting for you to come and collect your deed, but he keeps getting your money when there's no mortgage to put it against, because you don't owe anything.

Somehow, I imagine that's how God must feel when He sees us trying to pay for debts He already paid. Somehow, I imagine He is trying to shout from His throne, "Hey, honey, I've got you! It's paid for! You don't need to work that hard to try to pay for it. It's done and over. You're free. It's all good." Sometimes we're still in chains, working hard to pay for that two-bedroom mortgage. Freedom is the revelation, understanding, and acceptance of what has been paid for us.

> "It was for this freedom that Christ set us free [completely liberating us]; therefore, keep standing firm and do not be subject again to a yoke of slavery [which you once removed]." (Galatians 5:1 AMP)

Freedom is supernatural. It can be experienced only through Christ. There's no freedom outside of Him.

The word freedom is part of the complete meaning of the word *sozo*, sometimes translated as freedom, but often translated as salvation as well. We'll dig a little deeper into this word in another chapter, but the point here is that freedom can be experienced only through our salvation. It truly is a divine gift to be free.

> "It is my own eager expectation and hope, that [looking toward the future] I will not disgrace myself nor be ashamed in anything, but that with courage and the utmost freedom of speech, even now as always, Christ will be magnified and exalted in my body, whether by life or by death." (Philippians 1:20 AMP)

Freedom is to have Christ magnified and exalted in our whole beings.

We are three-in-one beings, spirit, body, and soul, and we must magnify and exalt God in all these three. To magnify Him in our body means not to disgrace it or do anything that would bring shame to it. Take good care of it.

To take good care of our body without allowing anything or anyone to shame us for doing so is freedom. We live in a culture that has shamed the human body in so many ways. I can't even begin to name them all. If people eat too much, they're called gluttons. If they don't eat enough, they're called anorexics. If they wear too many clothes, others think they're harming themselves. If they don't wear enough, people think they're showing too much skin. It's as if this generation lives trying to please people who are impossible to fully please, and in the process, they end up in a constant battle of never being good enough.

What feels right to you? What do you think is right for you and for your body in this season? Well, if you're right with God—and that is key—you're probably correct about what's right for you, no matter what the rest of the world says. And that is freedom.

The same goes for taking care of the soul. There's a taboo among believers that therapists are for weak people, and that all we need is Jesus. I agree that all we need is Jesus, absolutely! But while we're here on earth, God has said it is not good that we walk alone (Genesis 2:18). He created humankind for community, and we need other humans to help us grow and heal. Caring for our souls may well include help from professionals such as psychologists and therapists.

To seek the help you need without shame is freedom—whether that help is a therapist, a pastor, or simply a friend.

> "[Jesus][willingly] gave Himself [to be crucified] on our behalf to redeem us and purchase our freedom from all wickedness, and to purify for Himself a chosen and very special people to be His own possession, who are enthusiastic for doing what is good." (Titus 2:14 AMP)

Freedom is to be pure—to have pure motives in our hearts, a pure heart with pure intentions, free from all wickedness.

It's not our job to judge the hearts of others and determine if they're pure or not. We're to be concerned instead about our own hearts and motives. Keep yourself in constant check with God. If we give God permission, He will let us know if our motives aren't pure. Not in a shameful way, but just a little nudge to allow us to align ourselves with His motives.

> "In [connection with] all this, they [the unbelievers] are resentful and surprised that you do not [think like them, value their values and] run [hand in hand] with them into the same excesses of dissipation and immoral freedom, and they criticize and abuse and ridicule you and make fun of your values." (1 Peter 4:4 AMP)

Freedom is to have values that are aligned with heaven. When our values are aligned with heaven, God is on our side. There are no legalities or loopholes for the enemy to attack. When our values are aligned with heaven, our actions will be aligned also.

> "Therefore, do not worry or be anxious (perpetually uneasy, distracted), saying, 'What are we going to eat?' or 'What are we going to drink?' or 'What are we going to wear?' For the [pagan] Gentiles eagerly seek all these things; [but do not worry,] for your heavenly Father knows that you need them." (Matthew 6:31-32 AMP)

Freedom is to abide in His Word and be obedient to God's instructions for our lives. To live a life free from the common anxieties of this world because we know that the God we serve is a God who provides. Many may think that God's commandments are a prison. On the contrary, His commandments—His instructions, as I call them—are a hedge of protection from anything that could enslave us. When we abide in Him, walking on His path and following His instructions, we're free from all enslaving factors. It empowers us to live as saints and not as sinners.

Freedom is the understanding that salvation is not our destination. It's just the beginning. It's a ticket into the fullness of everything Christ has paid a price for us to have, a ticket into abundance in every area of our lives, a ticket to experience life on earth as it is in heaven.

> "So eat your meals heartily, not worrying about what others say about you—you're eating to God's glory, after all, not to please them. As a matter of fact, do everything that way, heartily and freely to God's glory. At the same time, don't be callous in your exercise of freedom, thoughtlessly stepping on the toes of those who aren't as free as you are. I try my best to be considerate of everyone's feelings in all these matters; I hope you will be, too." (1 Corinthians 10:31-33 MSG)

Freedom is to be able to honor God in each person regardless of their religion, beliefs, or race. Seeing God in them is freedom. Seeing them through God's eyes is freedom. We don't have to agree with everything they do to be able to love them and see them through God's eyes. Seeing them through God's eyes is honoring them.

We're all made in God's image. Some may be walking in His image and in their identity in Christ, while others may not yet be there. Either way, we should be able to identify character traits of God in others and treat them with love, respect, and consideration, not according to their behavior but according to who they are in God.

To love others unconditionally, regardless of how lovable they are in the present moment, is freedom. I call it free love. Because this love comes from God into our hearts for the people around us, it has little to do with the people themselves, and a lot to do with how free we are to love them.

Now listen to Paul's testimony and teaching about becoming free:

> "...I tried keeping rules and working my head off to please God, and it didn't work. So I quit being a "law man" so that I could be *God's* man. Christ's life showed me how, and enabled me to do it. I identified myself completely with him. Indeed, I have been crucified with Christ. My ego is no longer central. It is no longer important that I appear righteous before you or have your good opinion, and I am no longer driven to impress God. Christ lives in me. The life you see me living is not 'mine,' but it is lived by faith in the Son of God, who loved me and gave himself for me. I am not going to go back on that. Is it not clear to you that to go back to that old rule-keeping, peer-pleasing religion would be an abandonment of everything personal and free in my relationship with God? I refuse to do that, to repudiate God's grace. If a living relationship with God could come by rule-keeping, then Christ died unnecessarily." (Galatians 2:19-21 MSG)

Freedom is understanding that the grace of God is not for us to live in sin. On the contrary, the grace of God enables us to live a life of righteousness. It's important to understand that we don't have to attempt to please God in all we do in order to be loved; He loves us regardless. Don't get me wrong—I'm not saying we needn't bother to do things that are pleasing to God. What I'm saying is that we don't have to please Him to be loved by Him. It's not about our performance or about our own works. It's about His grace and His love.

He created us just the way we are, and He loves everything about who we are. We don't have to try to please Him. Instead, freedom is understanding that we get to live a lifestyle that pleases Him. Not a life of performance, but of holiness. We don't have to. We get to! Because His grace empowers us to do so. When we think we have to do something, we're automatically chained to our own limitations. But when we understand we get to do it because Jesus has enabled us, we're automatically free to tap into His infinite power and strength in which we can do all things.

> "Since Jesus went through everything you're going through and more, learn to think like him. Think of your sufferings as a weaning from that old sinful habit of always expecting to get your own way. Then you'll be able to live out your days free to pursue what God wants instead of being tyrannized by what you want." (1 Peter 4:1-2 MSG)

Freedom is to live for the will and purpose of God. It will always fulfill us immensely more than any desire we can have ourselves. While we seek our own desires and expect to get everything our way, we'll always have a gap—because we can be fulfilled only by entering our God-given purpose. The feeling of never enough imprisons us. But walking with God as He reveals His plans and desires for us each day frees us.

> "So be content with who you are, and don't put on airs. God's strong hand is on you; he'll promote you at the right time. Live carefree before God; he is most careful with you." (1 Peter 5:6-7 MSG)

Freedom is to live without worries. Freedom is to trust God, as we cast our cares upon Him and truly believe and trust that He has our best interest in mind. The cares and worries of this fallen world are too heavy a burden for any human to carry. It will make us tired and weary if we attempt it. But God has promised to be our caregiver! He promises to be "most careful" with us. Trusting that truth and letting go of the heavy burden is freedom.

Don't some of these definitions light up your spirit? Letting go of troubles, worries, and worldly anxieties, knowing that we have a God that cares for us, knowing that all we need to do is accept His love. How wonderful!

Perhaps some of these definitions bring you awareness and open your eyes to a perspective that maybe you haven't considered before—such as the fact that little white lies and supposedly "harmless" deceptions aren't that harmless after all. I'm sure we'll think twice before we tell a little white lie to our children again.

And it all sums up in one thing: Let go of ourselves and enter the liberty of being His child. Because He has paid the price for us and for our freedom!

Activation

Pray and meditate on this liberating and freeing psalm:
> Pile your troubles on GOD's shoulders—
> he'll carry your load, he'll help you out.
> He'll never let good people topple into ruin.
> But you, God, will throw the others into a muddy bog,
> cut the lifespan of assassins and traitors in half.
> And I trust in you. (Psalm 55:22-23 MSG)

A moment of gratitude:
Thank You, God, for Your freedom!
Thank You for having my back. And because You have my back, I am free, and I will not be shaken.
Thank You for Your promises.
Thank You for carrying the load for me! Thank You that it's never too heavy for me to carry, because You do the heavy lifting on my behalf.
Thank You for helping me out.
Thank You that I won't topple into ruin, because You are with me.
Thank You that I have Your favor.
Thank You that as I pursue my freedom, You have my best interest in mind, and You are on my side.
Thank You that I am free to let go of myself and my belief systems to embrace all Your truth—and the freedom and liberty of being Your beloved child!

Take the time to close your eyes and imagine that you're piling onto God's shoulder all your troubles, whatever they may be, and all your worries. As you pile them there one by one, feel your own load getting lighter and lighter, and feel the relief of removing the weight.

Allow His truth and His freedom to take place in your life now.

Take another moment with Him to just be.

Four

How the Subconscious Plays a Role in Our Freedom

"For freedom, Christ has set us free; stand firm, therefore, and do not submit again to a yoke of slavery."
Galatians 5:1 ESV

Galatians 5:1 is one of my favorite freedom verses. It says so much to me. Jesus paid the price and *set us free*. It is done. We must pursue that lifestyle of continual freedom and growth, and not submit ourselves again to the yoke of slavery.

When I first came to the United States from Brazil, I heard a testimony from someone in my high school. He used to be a drug addict, and Jesus saved him and set him free. He was free when I met him. His testimony impacted me. I wasn't yet a believer when I first heard him speak, and it sure planted a seed in me. He was a good guy. But years later, I'm not sure of the story's details, I guess one bad decision led to another, and this guy somehow ended up submitting again to the yoke of slavery—not only the drug addiction that once dictated and ruled his life, but also other addictions that might have been even worse. He lost his marriage, their beautiful home, and the ministry he and his wife had built together.

This man was free to do whatever he wanted. But somehow, he used that freedom for something worldly. At the end of the day, he ended up under the yoke of slavery because he didn't stand firm on the will of God for his life, on the true freedom he had. He failed to grasp why Christ had set him free to begin with.

I fully believe in this guy's redemption and restoration. God did it once, He absolutely can do it again, but it will take some decisions on his part, I believe, to bring him back to the place of freedom where he once was.

God hasn't left Him. This man didn't lose what God gave him initially. He just stopped living in that place of freedom and peace. He stopped pursuing his freedom and submitted himself to the yoke of slavery.

In this chapter, we'll discuss a brief example of a contradiction between one of the definitions of the world and a definition of the Bible for the word freedom. We'll explore how the misconception of freedom can put people back into the yoke of slavery. However, the main thing I want to discuss in this chapter is the power of our subconscious mind. It will be crucial to understand as we read the rest of this book.

It amazes me how some of the familiar definitions for the word freedom are pretty much the opposite of how the Bible portrays freedom. Incredible! No wonder we think we're free when so often we're slaves of our own wrong mentality. No wonder we're walking physically free while being mentally in bondage in so many ways.

Notice these two definitions from the dictionary:
- Freedom is the unrestricted use of something.
- Freedom is the power of self-determination attributed to the will; it's the quality of being independent of fate or necessity.

These are quite the opposite of what the Bible says freedom is. While the dictionary says freedom is to be unrestricted, the Bible explains that we can do anything we want, but not everything is convenient and fitting to us. As we understand that, making the right choice is complete freedom for us (1 Corinthians 10:23). To live unrestricted will ultimately lead to bondage, as we can tell with the story I told about the guy from my high school.

While the worldly culture says freedom is self-determination attributed to our own will, the Bible says freedom is submitting our will to Christ and being self-controlled. Self-control plays a massive role in pursuing freedom and standing firm in the freedom Christ has paid a price for us to experience.

Unless we have a clear understanding of what freedom is according to the Bible, and what those contradictions are, we may be going after something that's not only against the will of God for us but also against His freedom. And we can be deceived, thinking we're free.

According to neuroscience studies and research from multiple sources, only five percent of our daily thoughts are conscious and critical thinking. That means that ninety-five percent of everything we do is subconscious. It doesn't mean we don't know what we are doing, it means it's automatic. It's incredible to think that everything we do in our everyday, ordinary lives—working, going to school, loving our children, taking care of our families, supporting friends—is based ninety-five percent on decisions that aren't part of our critical thinking. Whoa!

I'm guessing you're beginning to catch where I'm going with this. How do we access this information, if it isn't part of the conscious mind? How do we do anything about it? Is our unconscious mind controlling our lives? Well, yes and no. No, because we have a choice, and that's what we'll talk about soon. Yes, in the sense that our brains are designed to save energy and put us on autopilot so that our conscious thinking is minimal, and our decision-making is "effective." The problem is that when our subconscious has a lot to be renewed and reprogrammed, our autopilot tuns into survival.

Our subconscious mind includes our beliefs, long-term memory, and protective reactions, which in turn are built around our belief systems and long-term memories, imagination, emotions, values, intuition, fears, and self-image. Our subconscious mind is responsible only for storing and retrieving information. That's it. It doesn't have any discerning. This has nothing to do with our spiritual giftings. It has to do with the design of our brain functions.

A perfect and extreme example of that is the Norwegian woman who lives as a cat. An intriguing article about her story was written by Jay Hathaway. The woman lives her life as if she's a cat, simply because she believes that way. That's her self-image in her subconscious. Her subconscious mind is trained to make decisions based on that belief system. It sounds absolutely insane, but it is not. She can sit down and discuss how she'll live the rest of her life being a cat. That is the power of the subconscious mind.

Our subconscious could be making decisions that lead us back into bondage, which submits us to the yoke of slavery we're already free of. And the only way to change our subconscious decisions is to upgrade our mental programming. Thankfully, that is possible—and that's what we intend to do regarding freedom, so that our choices will lead us to further levels of freedom.

However, that upgrade is a conscious process and requires intentional decisions. In the next couple of steps of this book, we'll learn a little more about how to shift some of the contents of our subconscious to replace the programming and make better automated decisions.

Not everything the world promotes is merely wrong; many times, those things are simply wicked. From the Bible, we learn that wickedness is present when the truth is contaminated with a little bit of a lie. A truth contaminated with a little bit of a lie becomes one hundred percent wrong.

Imagine you're about to get married, and your spouse writes his or her vows to you, and they say: "I promise to be ninety-nine percent faithful to you, honey!" No! That could be grounds for canceling that almost-marriage, right? Or at least for a very serious talk. "Hold on a second! Let's talk about that ninety-nine percent before we proceed!" I don't know about you, but I wouldn't enter a marriage knowing my husband is only faithful ninety-nine percent. Some things are meant to be all-or-nothing.

The same is true when it comes to definitions of important principles in our walk with Jesus, such as freedom. The one percent not aligned with the Word of God can take us the opposite way we were meant to go.

Therefore, my friend, we must truly understand the principle of freedom, because God intended us to be free indeed. I'm not here to tell you what to do or not do, what to believe or not. That's not my job at all. On the contrary, I'm here simply to share what I've learned. Please bring it all to God yourself, submit it all to the Holy Spirit, and see what applies to you and in what areas of your life.

One of the many things I've learned as I continually pursue my own freedom alongside the Holy Spirit is that it's not our job to convince other people that they aren't free in one area or another. We can't even do that for our own grown children, unfortunately. When we try to do anything for others that only the Holy Spirit can do, we open doors for the spirit of religion. So it's not my place to convince you of anything, nor is it yours to convince anyone else. I pray that the Holy Spirit will continue to unveil all His truth to us and continue to bring us freedom, because it's for freedom that Christ has set us free.

In this chapter, we understood that we were given freedom, and therefore, we must stand firm and not submit ourselves again to the yoke of slavery. And we understood that our subconscious makes most of our decisions, and the only way to change those decisions is to upgrade this process by changing its programming. We'll learn how to do that—don't worry!

Activation

Pray, and ask the Holy Spirit to bring to your conscious mind right now one thing where you've perhaps been on autopilot your whole life and didn't even realize it.

I could tell you many examples about myself, but one that rocked me is how I subconsciously transferred guilt. I didn't have the emotional capacity to deal with so much guilt when it came to my loved ones, so I subconsciously transferred the guilt to others when I was put in situations where I subconsciously felt guilty, as I've mentioned earlier.

The truth: I am not guilty. Although my choices may have affected people around me, those people are still their own individuals. They're fully capable of making their own decisions, and I am not responsible for them. Their decisions are not my responsibility. Therefore, the consequence is not my fault. Because of that, I don't need to guilt-shift. I can converse without feeling guilty about the consequences of their choices and simply offer advice.

That was extremely freeing to me. I know it may be a little deeper than you want to go. Or not! It's just an example to illustrate the activity. I'll leave you with the Holy Spirit now. Have fun.

Step II

PURSUING FREEDOM FROM A PLACE OF VICTORY

> *"For we are not fighting for victory.*
> *We are fighting from victory."*
> Dr. Tony Evans

We're fighting from victory because we're victorious in Jesus. He already won the war for us. It is finished. Done. Sealed in heaven. Victory, therefore, is where we stand. It's our starting point.

Freedom is part of this victory. Although we're pursuing freedom, we're pursuing something that technically we already have, because Jesus already paid the price for us to have it. Keep that in mind, and I'll touch on this subject again later.

There are four chapters in this step. We'll talk about the how, the what, and the when, which will be very practical and will give insight into reprogramming the subconscious. We'll then see how Jesus was free to love—and so are we. And we'll learn what it is that's trying to keep us from our freedom. Finally, we'll see that there is grace for our journey!

You'll continue to see activations after each chapter, which will help us practice the teachings, encounter Jesus, and experience the Holy Spirit.

Five

Because We Are Victorious, We Can! So...How, What, and When?

> *"Freedom is one of the deepest and noblest aspirations of the human spirit."*
> Ronald Reagan

Our former president Mr. Reagan got that right! Freedom is the deepest and greatest human desire.

From the time our kids learn to walk, we see them wanting to roam free and let go of Mommy's hand. As they continue growing, we see them searching for freedom to do more and more things on their own. They learn to feed themselves, to bathe themselves, and then—hold your hearts, parents!—even to drive themselves.

As adults, we continue to experience that constant need and search for freedom, yet whatever freedom we find never seems to fully satisfy. Couples end up getting divorced because they want freedom. Families split up and go separate ways in search of freedom, and churches seem to do the same. And the result? Most likely, we end up where we started—only now, a little more broken and alone.

We're born with a desire that seems almost impossible to satisfy.

In the beginning, God created us to be free. A desire and need for freedom were built into our DNA. God Himself is free, and since we were created in His image, we're created to be free—free to make choices and to be who God created us to be without restrictions or limitations. This is part of our God-given DNA.

But why would God create us with a need that can't be satisfied? Why would He engrave in our DNA such a desire for freedom that seems present from the moment we break out of the womb? This need seems to cause so much hurt and confusion.

The confusion isn't God's fault, however. The confusion is there because of our misconception of freedom itself. The confusion comes with the fall of mankind, not with God's creation of mankind.

As we explored earlier, the world's definition of freedom is more about independence than real freedom. And our independence has never been God's plan. He didn't create us for independence or give us that DNA. Independence is only a perversion of the original pure version of the freedom DNA that God gave us. He wants us to be free while depending on Him and on the guidance of the Holy Spirit in our lives. And that makes a huge difference. The desire for freedom that we're born with has been misinterpreted and corrupted for so long, we can't escape the results.

The good news is that we can reverse that corruption—and we will. As a matter of fact, you've already started this process through the revelations you had while reading the research on the word freedom. In this chapter, we'll continue to discover the pursuit of freedom—now from a place of victory.

The How

Let's begin to understand *how* we can fulfill the greatest intrinsic human need and desire—for freedom. True freedom, not independence. We discussed earlier how ninety-five percent of our choices are made by our subconscious mind, and we concluded that changing some of that programming would essentially begin to change how we live. Well, now we'll understand *how* to upgrade our subconscious programming to make better decisions. It's pretty simple—simple, not easy.

> "Do not conform to the pattern of this world but be transformed by the renewing of your mind. Then you will be able to test and approve what God's will is—his good, pleasing, and perfect will." (Romans 12:2 NIV)

Simple, yet very hard.

The Pursuit of Freedom

My sister is a neuroscientist, Dr. Poincyane Assis-Nascimento. She explains to me that our brains have pathways that are like expressways through which our thoughts travel freely and continually. Our previous thought patterns have built a well-trodden road winding its way through a thick forest. Building a new belief system and thought pattern is like paving a new and different pathway into an untraveled and unexplored forest. Can you picture that? Did you create a mental image of that new beautifully asphalted expressway versus breaking through the trees and bushes growing higher than you? I want you to create that image in your mind. Because now, to create a new belief system—to upgrade our subconscious programming—we must come out with a machete and make a new way through that wild and tangled forest, pioneering each step we take. And every time we think that thought again, we must be intentional about guiding that thought through the new pathway we're beginning to build, instead of allowing it to travel freely and automatically along that old, deep-rutted, beaten-down road that's been there for generations. And that's how eventually we upgrade our programming and build a new highway, straight and clear.

Once that road is built up enough to travel on, you must go back and throw some dirt on the old road to ensure no other thoughts will travel that way. Then put up a big "Road Closed" sign with an arrow that detours your thoughts along the new road you built. The process is simple, but labor-intensive and exhausting nonetheless. Not to mention the intentionality that it takes. However, the result is that you'll experience God's good and pleasing and perfect will on your new road. And that is freedom! Definitely worth all the hard work.

You can research books by neuroscientists—my sister should be coming up with something soon—on the renewal of the mind and get a much more in-depth version of my over-simplified explanation above. But that's it in a nutshell. I'm all for getting the full knowledge and explanation of things, but please don't try to overcomplicate things just because they are hard. Did you get that? Simple and easy are two different things. I find that humans sometimes try to overcomplicate things to subconsciously mask the fact that they don't want to put in the hard work to get the simple things done. Don't do that! Start putting in the hard work, and you'll see the results! The simplest things are often the hardest things to do. Simple does not equal easy.

What I love about the Word of God is that it's alive, applicable, and based on unfailing principles. Its principles, when applied, are guaranteed to work—so much so that you'll see people who aren't even believers following biblical principles and reaping great benefits from them. Why? Because the principles are unfailing. God is faithful to His principles.

The principle we're focused on here is the principle of the renewal of the mind. You renew your mind on the Word of God, you come out with new belief systems, and the result is that you experience and live out God's perfect and pleasant will for your life. This is what the Bible says. That's the principle, the application, and the result—the promise of Romans 12:2.

The principle of renewing our mind is the key to unlocking our freedom journey one step at a time. Each step builds on the previous one. Once we replace our old or broken beliefs about freedom with new, more accurate, and healthier beliefs, everything changes. Our choices and patterns of behavior will begin to reflect this belief change. It may seem awkward and perhaps unnatural at first. This new behavior is in opposition to our subconscious beliefs. As we exercise our new understanding by changing our decisions and behaviors, forcing them into alignment with our newly chosen belief system, it will become permanent. We'll change our subconscious, and transform our programming. We'll continue to do that over and over, and it will become a belief system to replace the old one previously established. We can consciously repeat this process in different areas of our lives in which we aren't living in complete freedom.

In essence, that's exactly what I did when I found myself in what appeared to be a complete lack of freedom that I mentioned earlier. When my world fell apart, I had to renew my mind about what freedom is, even more so than what I'd already done up to that point, and then seek further mental renewal about other things that were limiting me.

I suggest we can begin with the general concept of freedom. Depending on where you are on your freedom journey, you'll have more or less work to do. After that, we move on to other concepts or areas in our lives. By the fruit we see in each area of our lives—bad fruit or good fruit—we can identify the areas where we aren't living in freedom.

Sit with the Holy Spirit for a moment and choose an area of your life that you want help to analyze. Then simply ask Him for insight.

Examples of bad fruit might be a pattern of abuse in our relationships, or not being able to properly communicate our feelings and emotions, or not being able to be vulnerable—being unable to connect with others at a more intimate level, sometimes even with our spouses and children. Relationships are always a little more surface-level than what we would like them to be, and we just may not be able to pinpoint why or how to get it deeper.

Perhaps the bad fruit shows up as a need to control. We want to control the outcome of situations, or control people or their behavior. Maybe there's an extreme need to control your schedule and every minute of your day. Schedules are great, but the extreme need to control it may indicate bad fruit.

The point is that once we begin by replacing the general concept of freedom in our subconscious and begin the hard work of renewing our minds in that general area, we can then begin narrowing it down. There may be other areas where you already identify fruit that you don't necessarily like or want, but once you have the general freedom concept renewed, maybe some of those may just be straightened out without further work.

In the next section within this chapter—when we talk about the *what*—we'll discuss the single most important point to understand as a believer in order to be completely renewed. From there, everything else becomes possible. Though not easy! Remember the machete at work on a new forest highway. Not easy, but possible.

I know the Holy Spirit is already doing deep work in you by revealing and unveiling truths within your spirit that maybe you have never squarely faced. We must be humbly open for more revelation and unveiling of God in our lives. Application is equally important, but we could spend an entire lifetime with great activation and application of the wrong or incomplete truth if we aren't humble and open to the further revelation of His truth, leading us to the perfect will of God for our lives. Therefore, the combination of humility and application takes us furthest and fastest in our personal growth and relationship with Jesus.

The What

We understand—at least in theory—*how* we can be freer. If we're making choices and decisions based on our subconscious, then we must have a subconscious that's going in our favor and not against us, and we must make sure that our belief systems and deep understandings are rooted in the Word of God and not in some crooked lie we don't even realize we believe in.

Now the *what*. The first and perhaps most important step we must take in our freedom journey is to understand what happened on the cross. What is the extent of what Jesus died to give us?

When Jesus saved us and died for us on the cross, He didn't die just for our sins and to give us a place in heaven. That alone would have been enough! It is wonderful and amazing! But if that was all, the world could have ended, and we could all have just died right there and then, because the mission was accomplished. But there was more! There *is* more!

The Greek word often translated as salvation in the New Testament is *sozo*. It's a word that has multiple meanings, all expanding on what Jesus did for us at the cross. The word *sozo* can be translated as salvation, healing, restoration, and deliverance, and it has an even deeper meaning when put into context:

> "[Jesus] gave himself for our sins, that he might deliver us from this present evil world, according to the will of God and our Father." (Galatians 1:4 KJV)

I love this verse because it summarizes what happens when we're saved. We're delivered from this evil world, and we become free to live according to the will of God. Marvelous! Deep! You may say, "I thought to be saved is to be forgiven of our sins, free from the penalty of eternal death, and allowed to go to heaven." Yes—but there's more. Without a doubt, salvation is the most amazing miracle God has ever done. And salvation encompasses and includes so much more than what we commonly understand it to be.

Jesus gave Himself for our sins so we could be delivered from *this present* evil world—not just the evil world to come (eternal death). What is this present evil world? Whatever you think of that's evil in this world, Jesus died to save us from it. It doesn't mean that once we say yes to Jesus, we'll never experience evil again. It means that He opened a realm of higher possibilities for us, a realm with a superior reality for us to enter. A reality that is free from evil.

The revelation of this truth is absolutely astonishing to me. And it comes with our salvation. When we say yes to Jesus, we have access to heaven's reality, as we can see in Jesus's prayer model in Matthew 6, as He teaches the disciples to pray for the Father's will to be done in our lives on earth as it is in heaven. The reality in heaven is a superior reality. It's free of the evil of this present world that we live in, and salvation gives us access to that reality now—not when we die someday.

Too many believers have an incomplete understanding of what Jesus did for us through His death, burial, and resurrection. They believe it affects only the spiritual and eternal realm. Jesus also came to deliver us from this present evil world and give us a life of freedom and abundance here on earth. We're not just saved from hell, our sins, and future punishment; Jesus came to deliver, protect, and provide for us in this physical world.

To illustrate how rich the word *sozo* is in what Jesus did for us, let's look at some Bible verses and how that word is translated. Beginning with a couple of verses where the word translated as "save," referring to forgiveness of sin.

> "She will bear a son, and you shall call his name Jesus, for he will save [*sozo*] his people from their sins." (Matthew 1:21 ESV)

> "For since, in the wisdom of God, the world did not know God through wisdom, it pleased God through the folly of what we preach to save [*sozo*] those who believe." (1 Corinthians 1:21 ESV)

> "Wherefore he is able also to save [*sozo*] them to the uttermost that come unto God by him, seeing he ever lived to make intercession for them." (Hebrews 7:25 KJV)

There are also times when this same Greek word is translated as "heal."

> "And he [Jairus] begged anxiously with Him [Jesus], saying, 'My little daughter is at the point of death; [please] come and lay Your hands on her, so that she will be healed [*sozo*] and

live.'" (Mark 5:23 AMP)

Sozo in this instance refers to physical healing as well as resurrection from the dead. Jairus's daughter dies as the story unfolds, and Jesus raises her from the dead (Mark 5:35-43).

Sozo also applies to deliverance from demons:

> "They also which saw it told them by what means he that was possessed of the devils was healed [*sozo*]." (Luke 8:36 KJV)

Nobody could hold this man. He was known to be dangerous and uncontrollable. He often broke the chains that bound him. Sometimes, deliverance from demons is necessary for someone to receive healing and complete freedom. Great news! That is included in this word *sozo* and therefore included in our salvation.

Here's a classic example of Christ's saving power manifesting in our lives both as healing and as forgiveness of sins, with complete restoration:

> "And the prayer of faith will restore [*sozo*] the one who is sick, and the Lord will raise him up; and if he has committed sins, he will be forgiven." (James 5:15 NIV)

Sozo is also translated as "made whole" in reference to healing:

> "Jesus turned him about, and when he saw her, he said, Daughter, be of good comfort; thy faith hath made thee whole [*sozo*]. And the woman was made whole [*sozo*] from that hour." (Matthew 9:22 KJV)

In faith, this woman touched the hem of His garment and received healing. She was made whole. Here again, the Greek word indicating forgiveness of sin is applied to being healed physically.

This same healing, as recorded in the Gospel of Mark, reveals that just before this woman reached out to Jesus, she said to herself,

> "...if I may touch but his clothes, I shall be whole [*sozo*]." (Mark 5:28 KJV)

Salvation not only means forgiveness of sins but includes healing of the body and mind. It includes deliverance, freedom, financial prosperity, and wholeness. So many believers in the modern church have interpreted salvation to be only forgiveness of sin. Although that is included, it's an incomplete interpretation and understanding of what our Lord did for us. Christ died to purchase forgiveness of sin, our redemption from it, and from the consequence of sin, which is eternal death. That is true indeed. Yes, He did. And He also died to free us from all sickness, diseases, depression, poverty, lack of wholeness, and anything else that isn't part of our new being in Him—anything evil. He died to save us from the evil of this world.

Paul is clear concerning our atonement and our redemption from poverty:

> "For you are recognizing [more clearly] the grace of our Lord Jesus Christ [His astonishing kindness, His generosity, His gracious favor], that though He was rich, yet for your sake, He became poor, so that by His poverty you might become rich (abundantly blessed)." (2 Corinthians 8:9 AMP)

Jesus became poor so that we, through His poverty, might be made rich, abundantly supplied. Through Christ's death, burial, and resurrection, God has provided everything we need in this life and in the life to come—forgiveness of sins, healing, deliverance, freedom, and prosperity.

God is so good! He truly thinks of absolutely everything.

Salvation is the resurrection of the person God created us to be before the foundation of the earth, before the fall of man. It's the resurrection of His original plan for humanity. It is freedom! And it's available to every single human being.

> "Long before he laid down earth's foundations, he had us in mind, had settled on us as the focus of his love, to be made whole and holy by his love." (Ephesians 1:4 NIV)

> "For we are God's handiwork, created in Christ Jesus to do good works, which God prepared in advance for us to do." (Ephesians 2:10 NIV)

God knew exactly who we would be. He knew exactly what our strengths, gifts, and talents would be, and He carefully considered it all. First, He planned us, imagined us, and loved us. After doing so, He created the earth with us—His masterpiece—in mind. He created the earth to be a perfect atmosphere for us. Just think about this. He placed the sun and moon and all stars and galaxies exactly where they are to create the perfect atmosphere for us to live and thrive. This is mind-blowing; it puts me in awe whenever I think about it.

When the fall of man happened, it brought death to all the things God created us to be, all His plans for us. We were doomed to eternal spiritual death as soon as Adam and Eve ate from the fruit they were forbidden to eat. But God had a redemption plan to save us, and He sent His Son Jesus to Himself bear all our sins, to forgive us, save us, deliver us, heal us, free us—to *"sozo"* us! And when Jesus died at the cross, the fallen, old version of us died with Him. And when He resurrected three days later, we resurrected with Him, brand new! Victorious! The original plans of God for us were resurrected with Jesus. Our original identity was resurrected with Jesus, and He calls us His new creation in Christ Jesus. We're more powerful than ever, because now we know good and evil and get to choose good because of our love for Him. That is the position we stand in, and the place from which we pursue our freedom daily—*victory*.

Wow! I will always be humbly grateful for this reality. A reality that He gave us as a gift, for free—and it's available to anyone who believes and confesses it.

> "For by grace you have been saved through faith, and that not of yourselves; it is the gift of God, not of works, lest anyone should boast." (Ephesians 2:8-9 NKJV)

> "...if you confess with your mouth that Jesus is Lord and believe in your heart that God raised him from the dead, you will be saved. For with the heart one believes and is justified, and with the mouth one confesses and is saved." (Romans 10:9-10 ESV)

God has already done the hard work we couldn't do for ourselves. Our part is now simple: believe and confess it.

If, for whatever reason, you've never confessed it, go ahead and do so now. Confess with your mouth that Jesus is Lord, that He died to save you, and believe with your heart that God raised Him from the dead, and that with His resurrection, His plans for you were also resurrected. No matter what your past may look like, He resurrected the blameless, righteous, beautiful, perfect YOU. The *you* that was in His heart and mind before the earth's foundation.

I genuinely believe that if God can do a miracle big enough to save me from the kingdom of darkness I once walked in, bringing me to the kingdom of light, and using me to help others be set free—He can do anything. And this belief moves me each day. I pray you feel the same way.

Now we truly understand the *what*. Salvation is the ticket that gives us the right to begin a new life with Christ as a new creation, His new creation. It's a life filled with truth, life, and light! Salvation is not our destination; it's not the end. It's the beginning, the ticket to enter the rest of our lives as victorious humans. Salvation is the miracle that releases us to eternal life, and to a life of abundance that begins here on earth. Salvation releases the miracle of experiencing life on earth as it is in heaven. It's peace beyond human understanding. It's a higher reality made possible for us through Jesus.

Because we're free, we can stand victorious on our salvation, and we pursue freedom not as a victim fighting *for* victory, but as a conqueror operating *from* victory.

The When

When will we be free? Well, technically, we already are. The freedom we have in Jesus has already been paid for. It's already ours. What's left for us is to learn to live in that freedom, which I refer to as the pursuit of freedom, learning a lifestyle of freedom.

Gifts are not earned. They cannot be earned; they must be learned. This is important for us to understand, because we're not chasing after something that's running away from us. We're pursuing something from a place of victory; we're pursuing something we've *already won*. We often spend our lives trying to figure out how to earn the gifts that have already been given to us, when instead we must learn how to use and walk in gifts that are ours already.

Imagine buying a car for your thirteen-year-old son. It was a great deal. You knew car prices were going up, so you took advantage of the market and the deal, and went ahead and got your son the car, knowing that in only a couple more years, he would have a learner's license and would start learning how to drive. This car is already his—you bought it for him. There's nothing your son needs to do to earn it, because it's a gift. But he needs to learn how to drive before using his gift. And what if he decides to be a little lazy and not get his learner's license? Well, he's going to delay the use of his gift. Does that mean he didn't earn it? No, he didn't have to earn it. It's already his. But that doesn't mean he already knows how to use it. It's parked, with no use, because he doesn't know how to.

And what if he's super-motivated, gets his learner's license as soon as he turns fifteen, and learns quickly? Does that mean he earned his gift quickly? No, he still didn't have to earn it. It was already his. It just means he learned quickly and made good use of a gift he already had.

You get the point. Nothing your son did or didn't do changed the fact that he already has the car. Either way, he didn't have to earn it. Likewise, the freedom God gave us, the freedom Jesus paid a price for, is already ours. It was a gift. We didn't do anything to earn it, and we still don't have to do anything to earn it. We must learn it. We must learn how to navigate that freedom, walk in it, live in it, and drive it!

The pursuit of freedom is a life journey. Jesus has already finished His part; the work of the cross is done. Jesus is not going to die again! That part is complete. But *we* are not done. While we're here on earth, we're pursuing Him and the freedom and the life that He died for us to have.

We're growing from glory to glory. The journey, the process, and the learning equip us for each of the following steps, and for God's promises for our lives. If we walked straight into the promises without the journey, we wouldn't be equipped to stay there. It would be like the kid driving the car without knowing how. So let's enjoy our journey...the process...the learning...the growing!

Activation

This is going to be a multi-step activation, so take your time. Don't feel like you have to do anything. You are free! Do it at your own pace—if you wish, and as you wish. Keep in mind that all these activations are meant to engage your spirit with the teachings at a deeper level. It's not a task or to-do list!

- If you've never given your life to Jesus and declared Him as your Lord and Savior, or if you feel you need a "vow renewal," go ahead and do so now if you wish. In your own words, confess it with your mouth and declare that He has lordship over each area of your life.
- Review Step I and make a note of the worldly definitions of the word freedom that sound like freedom to you. Ask the Holy Spirit if there's any distortion with that definition, or any belief system attached to it, that needs to be replaced in your subconscious. Ask Him to help you see it from His perspective.
- Also in review of Step I and the biblical definitions, ask the Holy Spirit to highlight a couple of freedom verses for you. Make note of them. Ask Him why He highlighted them to you. Spend time meditating on it.
- Ask the Holy Spirit to help you begin the work of walking that new pathway in your mind in redefining freedom (upgrading your subconscious programming). Begin by reciting and meditating daily on the verses He highlighted to you. Do this for a few days until you feel led to go look for a new verse or to do something different.

Six

Because We Are Victorious, We Are Free to Love

"The Good News: Use your power and freedom always to remember to love those around you."
Adapted from Galatians 5:13

"I tell you to love your enemies and pray for anyone who mistreats you."
Jesus, in Matthew 5:44

When I was a teenager, my sister—who's three years younger than me—started dating a guy who was six and a half years older than her. I knew him from my high school, but he was even older than I was. She met him at my house, at one of my parties. (I had way too many parties.) So I felt pretty responsible for this relationship. Plus, she's my little sister, and we didn't have a father here in this country, so in my mind, it was my responsibility to protect her.

Since my sister was so young, my mother was concerned with the difference in their ages. We found out that the boy from my high school who she was dating happened to be the son of a couple of pastors who had come from Brazil to plant a church. My mother quickly found a way to get their phone number and began to call them to let them know how dissatisfied she was with the dating relationship between her daughter and their son. I drove my mother to their home to pick up my sister a few times, and helped my mother express her discontentment. Keep in mind that at this point, nobody in my household had come to the Lord yet, so the words we used and the way we spoke back then might not have been that nice—especially for me. I don't really remember the things I said, but let's just say I never had a problem expressing my mind out loud. Very out loud!

Years later, my sister married this boy from my high school—and he's now my favorite brother-in-law. I love him with all my heart. And through that relationship, our entire family came to know Christ.

But what I really want to share about in this story is his parents, the couple of pastors I mentioned who had come from Brazil to plant a church here, and who I probably mistreated again and again back when I was a teenager. They were most likely the people who, in addition to my mother and my sister, prayed for me and loved me the most.

I didn't come to Christ until years after my sister did. I was a little hardheaded, a little rebel. Throughout those years of rebellion, I had some rough times. That couple from Brazil showed me unconditional love in those times, in a way I'll never forget. They loved me when I was unlovable. When I was arrogant and deceived, too full of myself to see anything in front of me, that's when they loved me, cared for me, and prayed for me.

They came to my house to pray for my daughter, who was in so much pain from having one ear infection after another. I was desperate, and I didn't know what to do besides cry. She was allergic to the strong antibiotics, and no longer responding to the ones she could take. Her little body could no longer take any more medication, and she'd been having ear infections for the past six months. My health insurance was not yet active, and we needed to wait another six months before she could have her ear surgery. Imagine my heart as a new mom. I was devastated. But this couple, who are my senior pastors today, came to my house and prayed for her—anointed her—and she was pain-free until the day she could have the surgery. They came at other times to pray for both of my girls.

They also came to try to save my broken marriage, my first marriage. They loved on us, both my ex-husband and me. They simply showed up. They didn't expect anything in return. They didn't expect us to pay them, or to start attending church, or to give an offering or become members. No, they were loving. They were using their power and freedom to love. They were loving because they were free to love. They were planting seeds of unconditional love in me, though I didn't realize this back then. And I didn't see as clearly as I do now how important that was for me.

My life became a bigger mess as I continued to walk in deception and went through my divorce. I then met my amazing husband, who was an atheist at the time. Our lives were two messes brought together—two broken families, two very broken people. The couple from Brazil continued to love me, and now they loved my husband as well (who was then my boyfriend).

Jesus finally got hold of my heart. Not because someone gave me a list of religious rules, or told me where or when I should or shouldn't go to church, but because someone was able to love me freely, expecting nothing in return, when I didn't deserve their love. Those seeds that were planted by this couple—and also, of course, by my sister—finally germinated one day and became a sprout. All because someone didn't give up on me, didn't give up praying for me, knowing that one day God would do what only He can do.

And sure enough, He did! He always does. The little sprouts grew and became a tree that took such deep roots in me and is now an unshakable tree of unconditional love for others. I love people the way I do today because I was once loved the way I was then. And they were the ones who planted those seeds.

We all love because we were first loved by Christ. And it takes humans to express His love to one another and to plant those seeds—that's us, co-laboring with God. This couple were that for me.

Perhaps this is one of the most important things for us to understand—the value of genuinely using our power and freedom to love those around us. I pray that by the end of the chapter, you'll have it engraved in your heart, as we talk about Jesus's ability to love freely, as well as our own ability to do so. There's a level of freedom that we break through, allowing us to love freely. Please read that again, and let it sink in your heart for a second. Allow your whole being to meditate on that for a minute before you move on. There's a level of freedom that we break through that allows us to love freely as we continue to pursue freedom from a place of victory in Christ.

Jesus Loved Freely
Have you ever felt that you must hold back on loving someone,

maybe just a little bit, so that maybe you're not disappointed when the person hurts you at some point in the future? Maybe you do that by having some restrictions on your trust, affection, time, and how much you're willing to give to the people you aren't so sure about.

I'm not talking about healthy boundaries. We all need boundaries. I'm talking about putting up small glass walls between us and other people who perhaps God placed in our lives for a purpose, and we put up those walls because we're afraid of being hurt. The difference between walls and boundaries is the motivation of the heart. The motivation behind a wall is always fear. Fear of something. We may think it's natural, but is it really? Or is it that we aren't free to love without restrictions?

While Jesus walked the earth, He was the perfect example to follow; I think we all agree on that. And we see Him loving everyone freely! I cannot recall reading anything in the Bible about Jesus being judgmental or asking for some performance in exchange for love. Nor do I remember reading about Jesus loving with His guard up. When did that become a thing for us humans? Where did we learn to do that? Clearly, not with the correct source of love.

When I say free love or loving freely, I'm not referring to the love we have for our children, our spouses, siblings, parents, and the people we would typically love unconditionally; I'm talking about other people in general. I'm also not talking about abuse and lack of boundaries.

What I call free love has little to do with the person who's being loved. It has a lot more to do with one's ability to love without restrictions. It's not romantic love, not even friendship love; it's simply love. *Agape* love. The love Jesus has for us. It's not a feeling. It's a decision to be good and generous to others independently of how they act or react to us. It's a decision of genuinely desiring the well-being of others, desiring a favorable outcome for their lives, and not giving up on that heart posture. These decisions automatically generate in us a partnership with heaven in that person's favor, so instead of looking at them and noticing all their human flaws—which I'm sure they must have, as we all do—we look at them and notice them as God does. We're able to see qualities that God planted in them, and that perhaps they themselves haven't even noticed yet.

We could go over many examples of Jesus's free love in the Bible. One that really gets to me is His treatment of Judas, the disciple who betrayed Him—who gave Jesus up to be crucified. I'm not sure everyone realizes how beaten Jesus was. Have you watched the movie *The Passion of the Christ*? It's the one where Jim Caviezel portrays Jesus in the final hours before His death, and it includes a scene showing the Roman soldiers beating Him. It was brutal! And they say that what was shown in the film was only a small portion of the beating He experienced. No human being could survive that kind of treatment. Well, Jesus did. Because it was written that He would die on the cross, as He did. And Judas was the one who delivered him over to the authorities. Think about that. Jesus knew all along that there was this possibility that Judas would be the one to betray Him. Someone had to. It was written, and what had to happen, had to happen. Someone had to betray Him.

Knowing that one of His own disciples would betray Him, wouldn't you think Jesus would have some restrictions on His love for them, especially for Judas? Think about it. He knew someone would betray Him. Wouldn't you think He would maybe have some trust issues? I would! Maybe limit the access some of the disciples had to Him to guarantee no one was doing anything behind His back—as He tried to minimize betrayal possibilities.

Let's be honest for a moment here and think like rational adult humans about all the measures we could take to minimize betrayal and maximize our own safety if we were in Jesus's situation. Imagine you. Yes, you. You have a tight group of twelve students. People you do life with, people you trust, teach, and invest time and other resources in. These are people you love and have become friends with. They go everywhere with you. They speak like you, sound like you, and are like family to you. Then one day, you find out your life is at risk. You hear these brutal human killers are out to get you. You know it's your destiny to die, but that doesn't take away from the fact that it's going to be painful, or that you don't necessarily feel like dying.

The good news is that the killers don't know what you look like. It will be a minute until they figure out who you are. You got a breather there—or did you? You hear through the grapevine that one of your own people, one of your twelve friends who are like family, whom you love and cherish—one of them would betray you and turn you in. Your heart sinks.

That's heartbreaking. No, even worse—it's disheartening!

What do you do now? Do you call the police and have them all fingerprinted, maybe isolate yourself, spend some time alone, hire a bodyguard, and go somewhere with maximum security? Maybe hire a lie detector and have someone interrogate each of the twelve to figure out which one would betray you? Give them a speech? Tell them how you truly feel? You feel downcast! After all you did for them, how dare one of them even consider such a thing?

What else could you do? What if you knew which one was the traitor? Would you confront that person? Would you have that person killed or arrested, or at least contained in a place where they couldn't harm you before they turn you in to be killed? Would you put a restraining order against that disciple of yours? Would you be offended? Oh, so offended, for sure! That only makes sense, right?

But Jesus did none of the above. He loved Judas instead. He loved freely because He was free to love. He was destined to die on the cross. What had to happen, had to happen—it would come to pass one way or another. It didn't matter who would betray Him. What good would it be for Him to try to control the situation and change the outcome, when the ultimate outcome had been left in God's hands? And the ultimate outcome was that He died so we all could live.

What Jesus *could* do is control the attitude of His heart and the way He responded to pain and betrayal. And that's what He did. He responded with love. He loved Judas. Because He was free to love, He loved well. Wow! This is true freedom!

Jesus had all the rights in the world to make all the decisions you and I would probably have made two seconds ago when we imagined being in His shoes during the betrayal. He had every right because He *was* right. Yet He chose to give up that right, the right to be right, and surrendered to the ultimate plan of God the Father. And in that surrender, He served Judas alongside the other eleven disciples. He grabbed a towel, washed their feet, and they had their last supper together, a meal together. They sat, they ate, and they talked. Jesus chose to love on them, to love them all—even Judas, the one whom He knew would betray Him.

Jesus chose love. In the midst of pain, right before He died to save the entire world, He chose to serve and to love. This is the fullness of freedom.

Jesus didn't love Judas because Judas performed well and deserved to be loved. Jesus loved Judas because Jesus *is* love, and He is free to love.

You, Too, Are Free to Love
I can read this and other stories about Jesus's love over and over, and I'm deeply touched and incredibly humbled every time. He is truly the One and only Lover of our soul! Because He loves us so deeply and beautifully and freely, we, too, are free to love.

Before I had a relationship with Jesus, I didn't like people. I used to say I wanted to live on a desert island, and I wasn't kidding. I was deeply annoyed by other humans. I know this sounds horrible, but it's true. That was my reality before Jesus. I was even annoyed by my own person. So if anyone told me during my early twenties that I could have "free love" for people, I would say they were crazy. Such love did not exist in me. I said yes to Jesus when I was eight years old as I was being prepared to do my first communion. But I hadn't yet had an encounter with the person of Love; I hadn't experienced His love. And that's what makes the difference, I believe.

I know my heart toward people immediately changed the moment I had my first love encounter with God and rededicated my life to Jesus. Although I'm not sure when I started experiencing free love for others, I'll share with you the story of the first time I was introduced to the term "free love."

One day, I met someone in a retreat. It was a silent retreat; we didn't talk or exchange phone numbers, and I had no idea who that person was or what story was behind that person. I'd never seen the person before. As a matter of fact, I saw that person only twice during our stay—at the first moment, and at the last moment—but I had visions of that person during the entire three days we were there. Later, I learned that the visions I had were illustrations of what that person was experiencing during the retreat. For some odd reason, there was an unusual love in me for this person, and I knew it. I was able to recognize it. That love was not of my own.

After the retreat, I started getting words of encouragement and affirmation for that person, and I found a way to deliver them. I never once got a response. I kept on getting words, songs, messages and verses, and I kept on delivering them without a response. I would see this person every couple of months in different retreats, and I was told that the words were encouraging, affirming, and life-breathing when we saw each other in person before going into silence. For about a year and a half, I never heard a response from the person when I messaged. I was never offended or upset. I truly didn't mind that, because I was never expecting a response. I was simply being obedient to something I believed God had placed in my heart to do. And the free love in me for that person was still there and growing.

One day, as I was writing a message to the person, wondering where that uncommon love had come from, I heard in my spirit, "That is free love. It is My love for that person that I am sharing with you. You may choose to take it or reject it—and you chose to take it. I am glad you did."

That was awe-inspiring! Long before that experience, I knew that the love I suddenly had for people, in place of the annoyance and indifference I once did, had to come from Jesus. But this was my first experience with such uncommon love for a complete stranger. I felt as if I knew the person as a good friend—their struggles, their needs—and I wanted to help. After that, free love for strangers became more and more common to me. It's almost awkward—for the stranger, that is, not to me anymore.

Knowing God's love and His heart for people changed my life. In Scripture we read, "Whoever does not know love does not know God, because God is love" (1 John 4:8 CEV). This means that the more we know God, the more we know love, and the more we love as He loves.

Loving freely the way Jesus does is the most liberating and empowering place to be. We recognize that the way we choose to love has nothing to do with people's deserving or performance, but simply with our decision to love—and this puts us in control of ourselves, not of others. And honestly, if I can choose the single most freeing thing I've learned to do in life, it's letting go of the need to control others, and to instead control myself. The fruit of the Spirit is self-control, not others-control.

When we aren't free to love, we find ourselves trying to control and manipulate—even if subconsciously—people's actions, behaviors, situations, and outcomes. We do that to avoid hurt and disappointment. We think that if we can control the end result, it will always be favorable to us. We may be able to get away with that sometimes, and we may become really good at manipulation, but it's exhausting, and most likely we'll be disappointed. For the simple reason that at the end of the day, we were trying to control something we cannot control—other people—instead of controlling what we can control, which is ourselves.

When we bring all this into awareness and decide to love and to act in love no matter what, then all there is for us to control is ourselves. I'm not suggesting that anyone stays in abusive relationships or puts themselves in a place to be abused—*no*, by no means. But we can leave a relationship that's not healthy for us and still never lose our heart's ability to love. Because we control our actions and we have a choice, we are not the victims.

Jesus said in John 8:36 that whom the Son sets free is free indeed. We are free to love. We've been given the gift of freedom. It's now a matter of learning that gift and living a lifestyle of freedom. It goes back to the renewing of our minds, one thought at a time, one belief at a time, one stronghold at a time, until we're standing in front of a mirror and all we see is Jesus. And with our eyes fixed on Jesus, we are free to love! If we're able to see Jesus in ourselves so clearly, we'll be able to see Him in others, because we're much more critical of ourselves than we are of others.

I trust that your spirit came into complete agreement and alignment with the truth and the love that you just read in this chapter. I trust that as you realize and visualize Jesus's ability to love freely, you'll realize yours as well. As you pursue freedom from this place of victory in Him, you become more and more like Him, loving as freely as He loves—for it is His love in you for the people around you.

Activation

For this activation, I would like to do something you may think is a little unusual. That's okay! I think Jesus often did things many people thought were wild and unconventional.

I believe this is going to activate your freedom to love at a new level. It's an impartation prayer, so put one hand over your heart and one hand over your head, and repeat this beautiful prayer over yourself, adding to it as the Holy Spirit leads you. This isn't my prayer; it's Paul's prayer from the book of Philippians. I believe it was inspired by the Holy Spirit as much for us now as it was for the Philippians back then.

Imagine that you're receiving this impartation from Jesus Himself, the person of Love.

> "So this is my prayer: that your love will flourish and that you will not only love much but well. Learn to love appropriately. You need to use your head and test your feelings so that your love is sincere and intelligent, not sentimental gush. Live a lover's life, circumspect and exemplary, a life Jesus will be proud of: bountiful in fruits from the soul, making Jesus Christ attractive to all, getting everyone involved in the glory and praise of God." (Philippians 1:9-11 MSG)

Amen!

Seven

Who Wants to Keep the Victorious Ones from Freedom?

*"Even if our gospel message is veiled, it is veiled only to those
who are perishing, for their minds have been blinded by the god of this age,
leaving them in unbelief. Their blindness keeps them from seeing
the day-spring light of the gospel of the glory of Christ, who is the divine image
of God. We don't preach ourselves, but rather the lordship of Jesus Christ,
for we are your servants for Jesus' sake. For God, who said,
'Let brilliant light shine out of darkness,' is the one who has cascaded his light
into us—the brilliant dawning light of the glorious knowledge of God
as we gaze into the face of Jesus Christ."*
2 Corinthians 4:3-6 TPT, 2017

One of the pastors in our church taught this verse from a perspective I hadn't seen before, and the Holy Spirit brought me fresh revelation for this chapter as he was speaking. So I want to dig into this verse with you a little bit, because I believe it contains so many revelations about what's going on in the spirit realm in an attempt to steal freedom from humanity.

Knowledge is power. Once you have it, you can decide what to do with it. God once said, "My people are destroyed for lack of knowledge" (Hosea 4:6 ESV). And it's no different today, thousands of years later. We don't know what we don't know, and we perish for lack of what we don't know. But in this area, we'll no longer have a reason to perish, because the Holy Spirit is shedding light for us and bringing revelation knowledge that illumines our souls in a way that will lead us to a new level of freedom.

In the passage above, Satan is "the god of this age" who Paul is speaking of. Satan is described as such in various other New Testament passages, such as John 12:31 and 14:30, and in Ephesians 2:2. As the god of this age, Satan uses trickery, deceit, slander, accusation, and lies—among other dirty tricks—to blind people's hearts. The result of that blindness and deceit is unbelief. All unbelief comes from tricks applied by Satan. This blindness and unbelief keep people from seeing the light of Jesus, the burning fire of the gospel—the power it contains to transform us from the inside out and transform our lives completely into what God intended them to be.

The "brilliant light" that Paul talks about above in 2 Corinthians 4 can also be understood as a metaphor for spiritual revelation, the manifest presence of Christ, as we can interpret from these Old Testament passages:

> "The earth was without form and void, and darkness was over the face of the deep... And God said, 'Let there be light,' and there was light." (Genesis 1:2-3 ESV)

> "The people who walked in darkness have seen a great light; those who dwelt in a land of deep darkness, on them has light shone." (Isaiah 9:2 ESV)

Notice that the light God was talking about in Genesis 1:3 was not the sun nor the moon, for those were not created until the fourth day (Genesis 1:14-16). It was something else. A different light. A light completely set apart from anything that was dark. Both Revelation 21:23 and Colossians 1:15-16 suggest that the light is, in fact, Jesus's manifest presence. And it leads us to understand that darkness is not simply the absence of light; rather, darkness is a real thing. It exists, and in the very beginning, God separated it from the light.

The word translated as darkness in both Genesis 1:2 and Isaiah 9:2 is also used to describe ignorance—a lack of knowledge.

Satan, the god of this age and the enemy of our souls, will find areas of our lives where we have darkness—ignorance and lack of knowledge—and he'll plant lies, deceit, and tricks there that lead us to unbelief. Once we have unbelief in certain areas of our lives, we won't be able to see the light of Jesus in those areas. This will limit our ability to renew our minds and experience abundance and fullness of life. And that's how the enemy kills our dreams and joys, steals our hopes and plans, and destroys our relationships. He has no access to us directly, so he uses his dirty tricks to somehow infiltrate us, and he does it through areas of darkness and ignorance that will keep us from freedom. What a dirty trickster!

The good news is that once we bring light into darkness, darkness must flee. It cannot coexist with light, and light always wins. And bringing light (knowledge) into darkness (lack of knowledge, ignorance) is what we're doing now, so that you'll be fully equipped with not only revelation but also tools (your activations) to be able to practically apply this knowledge to daily life, and live in a higher level of freedom—whatever that looks like for you.

As we continue to pursue freedom from a place of victory, we'll review some of these tricks and possible areas of darkness in our lives so we can invite light into them. We'll also learn the importance of separating sin from identity.

What Are Some of These Tricks?
Knowing that the enemy uses tricks in our areas of ignorance to keep us in darkness and bondage, let us discover what some of these tricks are and remove his mask, so we can begin to shed light on some of these areas and completely dismantle these strongholds that Satan has created in our belief systems.

These tricks that the enemy uses are demonic influences, commonly known as spiritual strongholds. These strongholds can be rooted in fear, hatred, sexual sin, the occult, or witchcraft, or they can simply be generational.

Two major things open doors for these strongholds—one, coming into agreement with lies (often called limiting beliefs), and two, trauma.

Examples of limiting beliefs can include these things (as well as others):
— I'm not pretty enough.
— I can never get a degree.
— I'm stupid.
— I will never be anyone.

— I will always be a failure.
— I always find a way to ruin everything I touch.
— I wasn't born to be a good spouse.
— My father was an alcoholic, so I'll always be one too.
— My mother was a control freak, so I'll always be one too.
— This is just my personality, and I'll never change.
— Nobody likes me.
— I'm a mistake.
— I must do something for people to like me.
— I must earn people's love and respect.
— When I achieve all the things I want in life, I'll be happy.
— Men are all the same.
— Women are all the same.

Limiting beliefs can also come from trauma or your own perception of unworthiness—whether arising from things spoken by others or ourselves, believing hurtful things said about us, or religious and spiritual deception. Coming into agreement with lies, whether consciously or subconsciously, can limit our freedom in specific areas. You can see now why freedom can be something we pursue for a lifetime.

Trauma can happen to us at any time from our childhood on through adult life. Experiencing trauma can literally alter the neural structure of our physical brain. Trauma doesn't have to be something huge like sexual or physical abuse. It can include that, but it's not limited to it. It can be something simple, such as someone in school telling a kid that she has ugly ears or hairy arms. Bullying of any kind can create trauma.

Some examples of trauma:
— suffering losses
— perception of less worth
— physical or sexual aggression, abuse, or assault
— witnessing or suffering domestic violence
— natural disasters, such as a hurricane
— lack of any kind
— bullying
— neglect of any kind
— anything that destroys trust
— religious or spiritual abuse
— participating in or witnessing substance abuse

— abortion

— unsettling life events, such as a move

Trauma damages and causes changes to our insular cortex, which is a part of our brain responsible for the perception of basic pain and basic emotions like joy, happiness, anger, and disgust. The insular cortex is responsible for our relationship with our emotions. When our insular cortex is damaged, we have a different perspective of our own identity. We doubt who we are, and we have patterns of inconsistent behavior and undefined self-identity. I learned this from a pastor who also happens to be a neuroscientist; he leads the coaching academy from which I received my education and degree. My sister, who's also a neuroscientist and the smartest person I know, confirmed the information. So these are facts, not just some Google thing.

When I was fifteen, my mother moved from Brazil to Miami, Florida, with my two younger siblings and me. I was leaving all my friends back in Brazil, and I didn't want to move. Arriving in Florida, I didn't speak the language, and I had difficulty socializing. To say that I was unhappy and rebellious is an understatement.

In Miami, I met other Brazilians, but they were different. They weren't from the same city and social circle as I was in my country, they didn't go to my school, and they spoke English. Unlike me, they were familiar with how high school worked here. Because of all that, I felt like I didn't fit in. I didn't fit in with the Brazilians, although they spoke my language. I didn't fit in with the Americans, and I didn't fit in with the Hispanics. I didn't fit in at all. I had no place. I had no business being in this country. And when I spoke by phone to my friends in Brazil, I was out of the loop of what was going on there. I no longer fit in there either.

A belief system began to grow in me that I didn't belong. There was no place for me. No matter where I went or what I did, no matter who I talked to, I felt like a fish out of water. I grew up like that. This limiting belief was engraved in me until my late thirties, and I never realized how imprisoning it was, much less where it came from.

One day, listening to an audiobook, I heard a testimony of an immigrant woman from Ecuador with a similar story. That's when I realized how much bondage I carried in this area. I always knew I didn't fit in—that's how I felt in the business world, in school, in college, in the ministries I served, and sometimes even in my family and my church. This belief system was deeply rooted in me because of a stronghold caused by a trauma—a move. Granted, that move was the best thing my mother could have done for us. It gave us a life we otherwise couldn't have had. But the trauma happened nonetheless.

When I heard that testimony from the Ecuadorian woman, I realized where the trauma came from, what the stronghold was, and what the limiting belief was—and I simply came out of agreement with it. I understood why I always felt the way I did. I understood the feelings of inadequacy that had followed me my entire life. I simply choose to stop believing that, and I began to build a new thought pattern for myself from that point forward. Was it easy? No. But I knew what the lie was. And I no longer believed it. Light was shed into my place of darkness and ignorance. I began to pursue freedom from a place of victory.

I share this example because when we think of trauma, we often think of kids who grew up with some type of neglect or abuse—and yes, that does cause trauma, but trauma can sometimes have little to do with things that were spoken or done directly to us. Trauma can be caused simply by life events that happened and affected us—sometimes even positively, in the long run.

The great news I've learned from the Gospels is that God is willing and able to deliver and heal us and even to fix physical brain damage in the blink of an eye—and He wants to do that for us right now. If you've experienced trauma, I want you to know that whatever happened to you, it's not your fault. God never intended any abuse or trauma to happen to us. It's not His fault either. But there's one thing we need to be clear about. Although what happened to us is not our fault, it's our responsibility to move past it, to forgive, and to grow.

We're responsible for restoring our identity by renewing our mind, aligning ourselves completely with the new creature that we are in Christ, and pursuing freedom from the mindset that enslaves us. Freedom from victimism. And we do that from a place of victory that we already hold in Christ.

Until we learn to embrace this responsibility, all efforts to pursue freedom from certain strongholds are in vain. While we're blaming people or circumstances, we won't be able to take ownership of God's empowerment to move forward. And without His empowerment, we cannot do it.

We've learned to shed light on areas of darkness and ignorance, and in this way, we stand in victory as we pursue our freedom daily, destroying all strongholds that the enemy placed in our minds. We embrace the responsibility of becoming who God created us to be. *Free.*

Let's learn and grow together as we embrace this beautiful journey!

Separating Sin from Identity

A testimony from a friend:

> After a long sixteen-hour drive from Miami to Kentucky to see my family, I was approaching my hometown when I got the call. "Lori, it's happening. Be here for your brother, please." My mother's voice sounded desperate. My biological father was dying quickly of brain cancer. Thoughts rushed through my head at what seemed like a thousand miles per second. Everything from remembering all the things he'd done, how much he hurt me, and how long I'd waited for this day, to remembering the day the Lord saved me and adopted me into His family. I'd fully forgiven my father. So many emotions so fast. Then my mind pulled up something I'd forgotten. A few years back, I had a vision. It was me praying over my father with pure love in my heart. I knew the Lord was showing me through that vision that one day, I would be doing that. I remembered rejecting that vision. I remember not wanting that at all. Telling the Lord, I would never be able to love my father, that monster, enough to do that. I was willing to forgive him, but not pray for his freedom. I sat for a few moments and realized the Lord was telling me it was time. The time had come when I had to go and pray over my father.
>
> I began to drive to the hospital. On the way there, I tried to see if the Lord would negotiate with me. Can I pray *for* him instead of praying *over* him? I knew the answer was no. I needed to go pray over him, physically. I told the Lord I couldn't do it. But He assured me He would walk me through it. As I rode the elevator up to my father's floor, I told Jesus I couldn't do it. My body was shaking, and I couldn't breathe. He responded so gently, "You will not feel the sting of death.

When he says my name, it is finished." With that, boldness came over me. I stood outside my father's room. The man who destroyed my life, who I hadn't seen in eight years, lying there in his death bed just a few feet away from me—dying.

I walked into his room. My brother and nephew were finishing up with the hospital's chaplain. As soon as they exited the room, I understood it was my time to pray. I closed the doors and curtains. I approached my father's bed, lifted my hands, and began to pray fiercely. I was praying for my father's soul, not for his life. The prayer felt more like a business transaction. I explained how I'd forgiven my father, and the Lord surely had too. I asked for Him to allow me to bear my father's sin, that I would take the weight of his sin. I would bear it. The Lord said okay. He allowed me to feel the weight of his sin. The heaviness of what he'd been carrying. He then said I didn't have to carry that at all. He lifted it all like a vacuum. Because Jesus had already taken it all upon Himself, he bore it all already. There was no need for me to bear it. I felt a suction when the Lord removed what my father had been carrying. The entity and the weight that had been over my father his entire life, that kept him from being the father he could have been, and that instead made him the monster he acted out as.

A few minutes later, my brother and nephew reentered the room. My mother, sister, and I were quietly finishing in heavenly tongues. As we looked down, I saw my dad. My real dad. Love overflowed through me. This was a whole new man. I immediately knew I was looking at the man my father was supposed to be. Who he was born to be. All his sickness was gone. Not the cancer, but the perversion, the sin that held him down his whole life. It was gone. I got to see my true dad. He looked so pure. He looked so good. We stood around him crying, smiling, seeing the change with our own eyes, almost in disbelief, but in awe and gratitude. Moments later, we heard him say, "Thank you, Lord Jesus." At that exact moment, I knew, we all knew, it was finished. My father's soul was saved right in front of our eyes, and he was freed right in front of our faces.

After this, I was able to do things I never thought possible.

I was able to care for him, console him, and love him during his last few hours of life. In fact, I didn't feel the sting of death. I buried my father, who I love and am so proud to call my dad. I didn't bury the monster who hurt me and ruined my life, because that man was gone. I buried the man he was supposed to have been all along, his true self, separate from sin, a son of Christ. And I did that because Jesus taught me what it looked like to separate his identity from sin, and in doing that, he restored and freed not only my father but me as well, in more ways than I ever thought possible.

Wow! Isn't that a powerful testimony from my friend Lori? I know the Lord is still doing miraculous work in her because of so much freedom she has been experiencing from being able to love in this manner. That is why I purposely asked her to omit the details she wasn't ready to share, but to please share what she could, because it perfectly illustrates the separation of sin from identity. His entire life, her father lived in submission to an entity of sin that made him a person that he was never meant to be. And it destroyed his family, his children (particularly my friend), his marriage, and in the end, his life. The worst part of it is that he never realized it. He never got to live the life Jesus had for him, except for the last few hours. Because the deceived person doesn't know he's deceived. It could happen to any of us. This was a Christian man. I'm happy that in the end he rededicated his life, he was freed, and his family was restored in more ways than they ever thought possible.

Separating sin from identity is essential for us to be able to live the life Christ died for us to have. We separate sin from not only our identity, but from identity overall. Lori is pure-hearted and called to bring freedom into the spaces she walks into—allowing people to be who they are. Wouldn't it make sense that is what the enemy tried to steal from her? Likewise, the enemy wants to steal the most precious gifts God has placed in each of us. If she had not been able to separate her father's sin from his identity, perhaps he would have lost his salvation. And perhaps she wouldn't have experienced all the freedom she's experiencing because of what she witnessed.

What do I mean by separating sin from identity? When Jesus was at the cross, beaten and ready to die, and people were mocking Him, He shouted to God the Father, "Forgive them, Father; they do not know what they are doing." I see that as a great example of Jesus separating sin from identity. It's as if He was saying, "They have no idea I am doing this for them! To save their souls, they don't know who they are! They're acting like their sin, but that's not really them! That's why I am dying for them! So they can be who You, Father, created them to be—victorious!"

The mistakes we've made in the past do not define who we are in the present, or who we ought to be in the future. That's true for others as well. You may have been deeply wounded by others—even by parents or relatives, as my friend was. You may have been hurt by people you loved and trusted, people who were supposed to care for you and protect you. I'm sorry you had to go through that. Honestly, I am sorry I had to go through that as well. And I must say that their sin—their mistakes and flaws—are not who they are. Those things are not who God created them to be, even when they acted that way their entire lives, as was the case with Lori's dad. By no means am I justifying the behavior. I am simply saying we have the responsibility to separate sin from identity.

Here's a dictionary definition for sin: "an immoral act considered to be a transgression against divine law." In fact, an immoral act considered a transgression against divine law is also considered a sin in the Bible. However, the Bible defines sin as more than just that.

The first time the word sin was mentioned in the Bible, it wasn't referring to a mistake or a transgression of a law:

> "If you do well [believing Me and doing what is acceptable and pleasing to Me], will you not be accepted? And if you do not do well [but ignore My instruction], sin crouches at your door; its desire is for you [to overpower you], but you must master it." (Genesis 4:7 AMP)

Sin is not a verb there, but a noun, an entity. The Bible first refers to sin as an entity that crouches at our door, and we must master it. As a matter of fact, the Bible refers to sin a lot more often as an entity than as an action or a verb. It's an entity, and in Genesis 4, it's separate from Cain—who, under an inferior covenant, was already able to master it, according to God Himself.

When sin first encountered humans, it brought shame and fear into God's perfect paradise. It came in with a lie that questioned the human identity and God's goodness toward humanity:

> "For God knows that on the day you eat from it your eyes will be opened [that is, you will have greater awareness], and you will be like God, knowing [the difference between] good and evil." (Genesis 3:5 AMP)

Still today, that's the same strategy the enemy uses against us. He questions our identity and our trust in God's good intentions toward us. And when we fall for that, we identify with sin and begin to live from that perspective. When we do that, we believe we're a mistake, and we judge and label ourselves and the people around us accordingly. The result is constant disappointment, discouragement, and disbelief. As we identify more with that entity than with ourselves, we begin to live as if that was our identity.

We must understand that the sinful nature is not in us. It's a separate entity that comes against us to steal, kill, and destroy what Christ has paid a price for us to have: freedom. That sinful nature is an unwelcome intruder, a deceiving spirit that speaks in our minds in such a convincing way that we think it *is* us. It's time we separate that entity of sin from who we are, and do the same for people around us. We are not a mistake. We make mistakes, but those things don't define who we are. The wrong and impure thoughts and desires are not who we are. It is sin speaking in our ears, just as it did to Eve back in the garden of Eden. This sin is *against* us. It is our enemy. It wants us dead, spiritually dead.

When we stand in God's unshakable and unmovable truth, we understand that we do not fight *for* victory but *from* victory—the victory Christ already won for us at the cross. We are not fighting to win the war. The war is already won! We pursue freedom from a place of victory!

I certainly pray that you can understand the importance of separating sin from identity, for yourself as well as for those around you.

Activation

What I like to do for this activation is something very practical. I like to name the voices in our heads, the entity of sin. Give it a name, whatever name you want. Then, let's practice recognizing its voice. When you think you're hearing its voice, call its name and tell it to shut up. It's amazing how effective it is to name this entity something and call it what it is, instead of accepting its voice as your own.

Some tips:
— That entity can come against you in different ways and sound different every time.
— One thing it always has in common: whatever it tells you never adds to who you are.
— It is always against you, never in you.
— Go ahead, give it a name. Call it Lola or Koko, or whatever name you want.
— You'll hear it as thoughts most of the time: "It's okay to call my ex-boyfriend." Or, "My husband acted like a jerk." Or, "Just a little white lie never hurts anyone." You call its name and tell it to shut up.

You speak the truth about who you are: "I am honorable, so I honor my husband, because that's who I am." And, "I speak the truth. I am a child of truth."

As you become aware of how much the entity of sin talks, you'll be able more and more to separate it from who you are, to call it by name, and to deny its authority in ruling your life.

You are a child of the King! You're part of a royal priesthood, bound to win, destined for glory and freedom! That has already been decided and established about you! And now, you're empowered to live it out.

Eight

Because We Are Victorious, There Is Grace for the Journey

*"God, I invite your searching gaze into my heart.
Examine me through and through.
Find out everything that may be hidden within me.
Put me to the test and sift through all my anxious cares.
See if there is any path of pain I'm walking on,
and lead me back to your glorious, everlasting ways—
the path that brings me back to you."*
Psalm 139:23-24 TPT, 2017

One day a while back, I prayed this psalm, as I do often. I love this translation of this psalm. Other translations usually say, "sinful way in me" or "offensive way," but this translation says "path of pain." Ultimately, when we walk in sin or in ways that are offensive to the Holy Spirit in us, even if we're unaware of it, it causes pain within us. It becomes a path of pain in our lives.

This day, I was praying that psalm, and I almost immediately heard in my heart the answer to my prayer. I saw clearly what my path of pain had been. And this is what I perceived:

> "Idolatry of self comes from a place of striving to live for God. It sounds contradicting, I know. But that lifestyle brings us to a place of elevating the things we do for God into the center of our hearts, and the center of our hearts is a place that belongs to Jesus alone. What pleases God is us being with Him and doing life with Him, and everything else should come from

that. When we try so hard to live for Him and do everything we do for Him, subconsciously we go into performance mode. Performance is a perversion of the real us. The real us doesn't require striving or working hard to be. The real us is just us with God at the center. Performance brings self to the center instead of God."

And if I may add, even the pursuit of freedom cannot come into the center of our heart in the place of Jesus or along with Him. The center of our hearts is for Jesus and Jesus only.

That day, I saw in the Spirit that He was wiping clean a white canvas. I understood that He was giving me the opportunity to bring Him to the center of my heart so that I could grow to the next level of glory, with the awareness of what's really at the center of my heart and my life. I believe He does that for all who believe and receive. He wipes clean the canvas of our path of pain and brings us to His glorious and everlasting ways.

I recently prayed this psalm again, and I had another beautiful experience. I had a revelation of His grace resting upon the life of His victorious bride. And I heard in my spirit these lovely words: "Because you are victorious, there is grace for your journey."

God's grace for our lives and journey is more profound than I can put into words. It is more than unmerited favor. It is God's empowering presence that enables us to become the person He sees when He looks at us. It enables us to live and be who He created us to be in Christ, free and victorious. Without shame and without fear. Without the need to pretend. Without the need to perform or to strive. Free to be who we are. Growing from glory to glory, from grace to grace, by His grace, in His grace. Pursuing freedom from a place of victory. We don't have to worry about who we were, who we will be, or what's coming our way. With God's grace upon us, there's grace for our journey, and that grace allows us to live our lives as worship unto Him, one step at a time. That grace allows us to stand victorious, knowing that He fills our gaps. He is the great I Am, and in our weakness, He is strong!

> "What shall we say [to all this]? Should we continue in sin and practice sin as a habit so that [God's gift of] grace may increase and overflow?" (Romans 6:1 AMP)

What is Paul talking about in this verse? What is "all this"? What is he referring to? He's referring to the poor human condition that people were living in. A condition of habitual sin, living as if there was no Savior and no future. It's almost like the popular teenage saying "YOLO"—you only live once. They took it as doing whatever you want, letting sin superabound, because there's only one chance to do all these wrong things our flesh may want to do here on earth. If God said He forgave it already, let's take full advantage of it.

> "Certainly not! How can we, the very ones who died to sin, continue to live in it any longer? Or are you ignorant of the fact that all of us who have been baptized into Christ Jesus were baptized into His death? We have therefore been buried with Him through baptism into death, so that just as Christ was raised from the dead through the glory and power of the Father, we too might walk habitually in newness of life [abandoning our old ways]." (Romans 6:2-4 AMP)

If grace is superabundant when sin is superabundant, then should we sin more so that we're able to witness more grace? Obviously not. That's not the point of grace at all! That's what Paul is saying here, which is still the answer for us today.

I usually tell my youngest daughter, "Yolo, honey. You get only one chance to do your best here on this earth. Make sure you take full advantage of every opportunity." And maybe that has reframed that popular saying for her. The reality is that grace empowers us to live away from sin, away from the entity that once enslaved us and terrorized us, and we should not submit ourselves back into it.

With the fall of Adam and humanity with him, the entity of sin had dominion over us, and that's when our identities became entwined with sin's identity, because its nature became human nature, as described back in Genesis 6 when the Lord grieved having created humankind because of how evil its nature had become. But He had a solution, a redemptive plan. Once we accept that plan—Jesus's sacrifice for us, and the price He paid at the cross to take upon Himself that old sinful nature in exchange for His holy nature—that old sinful nature no longer has power or authority over us. This is the essence of the gospel of freedom.

Grace empowers us to live in freedom and pursue freedom in every area of our lives from a place of victory—the victory we already have in Jesus. Let's go back now and talk a little more about pursuing something we already have.

Consider your spouse. You're already married. Technically, you already have your partner, correct? However, you want to pursue that partner for the rest of your life. By doing that for each other, you'll make sure you're always aware of each other's needs, emotions, likes, and desires, which will change over time. You'll keep your relationship alive, and that feeling of butterflies in your stomach that you had when you first started dating will happen again every once in a while. As you pursue your lifelong partner, you'll continually learn new things about them because human beings are complex creatures. There will always be something new to discover.

Pursuing freedom can be like pursuing a lifelong partner. You already have it, but that relationship is constantly growing and evolving and manifesting in new, beautiful, and different ways.

On the other hand, what happens if you get married, and instead of continually pursuing your spouse, you go back to living your life as if you were still single? Well, that may not work out, right? The fact that you chose to get married came with a package of choices that brought some responsibilities and privileges exclusive to married people. And the same is true for your spouse. It's not a matter of control; it's a matter of love and respect.

The same can be said about your pursuit of freedom. Although you can do all things, not all things are convenient and favorable to you. There are some responsibilities and privileges that are exclusive to those who are free, and we must choose well as we continually pursue freedom from a place of victory, empowered by the grace that God gives us for our journey.

Our continual pursuit of Jesus, the source of all our freedom, will always lead us to deeper freedom in different areas of our lives. The more we believe in the promises He made for our lives, the more freedom we'll experience from the temporary reality of this fallen world. Please read that again. That is faith, and faith doesn't always make sense rationally, yet it makes all the sense in the world for those who believe.

I was in one of my times of silence when God spoke to my spirit, and I understood He was depositing in me a new portion of grace.

In that place of grace, He began to give me a fresh understanding of the gradual process of freedom, and I understood that there's a new portion of grace to take us forward to each level of glory and each level of freedom. He gave me a fresh insight into John 8:32, where Jesus says, "You will know the truth, and the truth will set you free." When you know the truth of the Word of God, it unveils for you a superior reality. The word *truth* here in this verse represents *reality*. However, maybe you adopt that reality only in stages. Each time you recognize that reality a little more and make it *your* reality, you're a little further along in your journey of freedom in that area. Freedom comes according to your level of belief and how you perceive truth and understand that reality to be your own.

This is profound. Take some time to meditate on it, and allow the Holy Spirit to take it from your head to your heart.

To know that He gives us a new level of grace for each level of glory is extremely comforting and empowering. We're fully dependent on Him, yet fully free to pursue this wild freedom He desires for us to live.

That has been His desire from the very beginning. All that's left for us to do is give Him our undaunted, unapologetic *yes*. Yes, Lord, I say yes to Your heart, and yes to Your freedom.

As we continue to pursue His freedom from a place of victory, there's a new level of grace for each step of the way.

Activation

In this activation, I encourage you to pray the prayer in Psalm 139 that King David prayed, and which I love to pray and meditate on. Seek God for His path to glorious and everlasting ways!

> God, I invite your searching gaze into my heart.
> Examine me through and through.
> Find out everything that may be hidden within me.
> Put me to the test, and sift through all my anxious cares.
> See if there is any path of pain I'm walking on,
> and lead me back to your glorious, everlasting ways—
> the path that brings me back to you. (Psalm 139:23-24 TPT, 2017)

Spend some time in His presence, capturing any thoughts you may have, and journal them. You have the mind of Christ, and you're in a time of quietness with the Holy Spirit. The thoughts you're having most likely is a conversation between you and God in your spirit! Do not dismiss it.

The more you have these "conversations," the better you'll learn to quickly identify them and distinguish God's voice from your own.

Step III

PURSUING FREEDOM FROM A PLACE OF IDENTITY

*"My old identity (my old nature) has been co-crucified with Messiah
and no longer lives; for the nails of his cross crucified me with him.
And now the essence of this new life is no longer mine,
for the Anointed One lives his life through me—we live in union as one!
My new life is empowered by the faith of the Son of God
who loves me so much that he gave himself for me,
and dispenses his life into mine!"*
Galatians 2:20 TPT, 2017

I said yes to Jesus as a child during my first communion. It was part of what we did in preparation for the ceremony. But it was during my late twenties, when I rededicated my life and began a relationship with Him, that I became aware of the Holy Spirit in me. I believe that's truly what makes a difference.

I believed in Jesus. I always did. But the Bible says that even demons believe in Him and tremble! (James 2:18-20). What's the difference, then? I believe it is *knowing* Him and developing a relationship with Him. And through knowing Him, we come to know ourselves and come into agreement with the work He did at the cross for us, and with who we are in Him. Not because of ourselves and our own works that we could boast, but because of His grace, and His faith, that empowers us.

The day I committed my life to Christ, I had an incredible experience. It was after a Bible study. There was an altar call that I couldn't get up for because my niece was sleeping on my lap. So I stayed in my seat, but I knew that call was for me, and in my seat, I quietly prayed and surrendered my life to Jesus. I was in a bad place at work, and I must confess that at that time, work was governing my life. It was my source. And I'd heard God give me specific solutions and instructions during that Bible study. It was my first time attending a Bible study, and I was blown away by how productive it had been for me at a personal level. So I knew that altar call was for me.

As I began to talk to God in my seat, I had a vision right in front of my open eyes. I was being crucified with Jesus, nailed to the cross. I was dying. Except nothing was hurting me. Then I saw myself standing in front of Him as He resurrected, in a place I didn't know but looked like an illustration from a history book. He exchanged something from His inside for something that had been in my inside. I heard Him say some words to me—I remember what they were, but I didn't understand them at the moment, any more than I understood the vision I was seeing.

From that day forward, I began to attend Bible studies frequently, as well as church services, and I began to study the Bible on my own, guided by the Holy Spirit. I began to research symbols in my vision and in the things I heard in that vision. One day, I came across this verse, and I began to understand what had happened:

> "I have been crucified with Christ [that is, in Him I have shared His crucifixion]; it is no longer I who live, but Christ lives in me. The life I now live in the body I live by faith [by adhering to, relying on, and completely trusting] in the Son of God, who loved me and gave Himself up for me." (Galatians 2:20 AMP)

This is—as I'm sure you've noticed—the same verse I quoted above in a different translation. I still didn't fully understand it; it was just the beginning. But I realized that the vision I had was an illustration of this verse.

Nowadays, I can fully comprehend that it was so much more than just an illustration. God allowed me to see what Jesus did on the cross not only for me but for all of us. Jesus didn't just die for us, He died *as* us. And when He resurrected, He exchanged our old sinful nature for His nature. And we were born again as new creatures in Him. We no longer live the same lives, but a new life in Him—the one He gave us from inside Himself, in exchange for the one He took from us.

God is outside time, and so is our spirit. The vision I had that day was as if He took me back to the day of His crucifixion, and then His resurrection, and allowed me to be there, seeing what was happening and how I played a part in it, as well as the rest of the believers.

Believe me, to say I was undone by this understanding is an understatement.

This step of pursuing freedom from a place of identity is all about you, coming into agreement with what Jesus did for you at the cross, coming into agreement with your identity and who you are in Him, and pursuing freedom from that place of identity—that place of knowing who you are. I want to invite you into my vision and picture yourself there, in that verse, on that cross, being crucified with Jesus and then resurrected with Him, as He exchanges His perfect nature for the old fallen nature you used to have.

Nine

You Are Free of a Sinful Nature

*"Therefore, if anyone is in Christ,
the new creation has come:
The old has gone, the new is here!"*
2 Corinthians 5:17 NIV

I once had an experience where I was helping someone find freedom in God, and I heard in my spirit some specific instructions for her. She was to push her old self down the cliff and embrace her new self. That may sound silly, but sometimes it takes a physical act of obedience to release something in the supernatural realm. Like Moses, when he needed to stretch out his hands to open the Red Sea. Or the priests, when they needed to touch the Jordan River with their toes at the edge of the water for the flow to stop. And many other examples the Bible offers us.

She did it. And it released something supernatural. What happened after that is between her and the Lord, it's not for me to share, but it sure released something supernatural in the spirit realm.

The truth is that we are in Christ, and we're a new creation. The old has gone. Down the cliff, drowned in the ocean. However you want to picture it, it doesn't really matter. It matters that you know you're a new creation.

What does it mean to be a new creation? What does it mean not to have a sinful nature? What is a sinful nature, and what is Christ's nature?

I'll answer these questions in quick bullet points, for quick clarification. But I know that throughout this book, even in the previous step, you've already picked up clues that answer these questions, and

you may not even need these answers. But here they are:
- That word *new* in the verse above means *never made before, fresh, new in species and character, better and of higher excellence*. To be a new creation means that you've been redeemed from the curse of the fall and not just *fixed*, but remade to be better than ever before.
- The sinful nature is what God refers to back in Genesis 6, when He grieved making humans, because the intentions of human hearts were evil. The sinful nature came with the fall, and it's a nature that has an evil inclination.
- Christ's nature is God's nature, since Christ is God, and He came to illustrate God's invisible nature, as is stated in Colossians 1:15-16. Above all, His nature is love—and justice, purity, holiness, beauty, patience. We cannot name it all. But one thing is certain. It is one hundred percent good.
- When we accept Jesus in our life, we become the temple of God. There's an exchange that takes place, and that's the concept of being born again. He exchanges our old sinful nature for His nature, which becomes our new nature. The Holy Spirit comes in to replace the old, which from that point on, no longer lives in us. It's a heavenly transaction, an exchange that happens in the spirit realm the second we accept Jesus's sacrifice for us and accept Him as our Lord and Savior.

Now, because we no longer have a sinful nature, does that mean we're unable to sin or to make mistakes? No, it doesn't mean that. What it means is that sin is no longer our inclination. Sins and mistakes do not define who we are, and neither do the mistakes we've made in the past. We may have sinned, but that doesn't make us a sinner. We may have cheated, but that doesn't make us a cheater. We may have lied, but that doesn't make us a liar. You get the point. Jesus defines who we are because we have His nature.

This is not a green light to live in sin. On the contrary, because of God's grace for us, we're now empowered to live a righteous life that glorifies Him. God has already forgiven us. Who we are is not attached to what we've done. We must forgive ourselves, and forgive others who've done wrong against us as well. The grace of God empowers us to leave our mistakes and the mistakes of others behind, and to step up to the fullness of who He created us to be.

I understand this may be a contradictory topic for you. You may have grown up believing that you're a sinner saved by grace. So please don't take my word for it, but study the Bible for yourself. It may require you to give up some of your desire to be right and to instead embrace a deep want for the truth. A pastor I know often says, "Repeat after me: I don't need to be right; I just need to know the truth." So please repeat that out loud. It's very freeing.

Here are some scriptures, but please search for more on your own as well.

> "Do you not know that your bodies are members of Christ? Am I therefore to take the members of Christ and make them part of a prostitute? Certainly not! Do you not know that the one who joins himself to a prostitute is one body with her? For He says, "The two shall be one flesh." But the one who is united and joined to the Lord is one spirit with Him. Run away from sexual immorality [in any form, whether thought or behavior, whether visual or written]. Every other sin that a man commit is outside the body, but the one who is sexually immoral sins against his own body. Do you not know that your body is a temple of the Holy Spirit who is within you, whom you have [received as a gift] from God, and that you are not your own [property]? You were bought with a price [you were actually purchased with the precious blood of Jesus and made His own]. So then, honor and glorify God with your body." (1 Corinthians 6:15-20 AMP)

> "Do you not know and understand that you [the church] are the temple of God, and that the Spirit of God dwells [permanently] in you [collectively and individually]? If anyone destroys the temple of God [corrupting it with false doctrine], God will destroy the destroyer; for the temple of God is holy (sacred), and that is what you are." (1 Corinthians 3:16-17 AMP)

> "Do not be unequally bound together with unbelievers [do not make mismatched alliances with them, inconsistent with your faith]. For what partnership can righteousness have with lawlessness? Or what fellowship can light have with darkness? What harmony can there be between Christ and

Belial (Satan)? Or what does a believer have in common with an unbeliever? What agreement is there between the temple of God and idols? For we are the temple of the living God; just as God said:
'I will dwell among them and walk among them;
and I will be their God, and they shall be My people.
So come out from among unbelievers and be separate,' says the Lord,
'and do not touch what is unclean;
and I will graciously receive you and welcome you [with favor],
and I will be a Father to you,
and you will be My sons and daughters,'
says the Lord Almighty." (2 Corinthians 6:14-18 AMP)

"So then you are no longer strangers and aliens [outsiders without rights of citizenship], but you are fellow citizens with the saints (God's people), and are [members] of God's household, having been built on the foundation of the apostles and prophets, with Christ Jesus Himself as the [chief] Cornerstone, in whom the whole structure is joined together, and it continues [to increase] growing into a holy temple in the Lord [a sanctuary dedicated, set apart, and sacred to the presence of the Lord]. In Him [and in fellowship with one another] you also are being built together into a dwelling place of God in the Spirit." (Ephesians 2:19-22 AMP)

"You [believers], like living stones, are being built up into a spiritual house for a holy and dedicated priesthood, to offer spiritual sacrifices [that are] acceptable and pleasing to God through Jesus Christ." (1 Peter 2:5 AMP)

"Therefore if anyone is in Christ [that is, grafted in, joined to Him by faith in Him as Savior], he is a new creature [reborn and renewed by the Holy Spirit]; the old things [the previous moral and spiritual condition] have passed away. Behold, new things have come [because spiritual awakening brings a new life]." (2 Corinthians 5:17 AMP)

"Do not lie to one another, for you have stripped off the old self with its evil practices, and have put on the new [spiritual] self who is being continually renewed in true knowledge in the image of Him who created the new self—a renewal in which there is no [distinction between] Greek and Jew, circumcised and uncircumcised, [nor between nations whether] barbarian or Scythian, [nor in status whether] slave or free, but Christ is all, and in all [so believers are equal in Christ, without distinction]." (Colossians 3:9-11 AMP)

"Set your mind and keep focused habitually on the things above [the heavenly things], not on things that are on the earth [which have only temporal value]." (Colossians 3:2 AMP)

"Therefore we do not become discouraged [spiritless, disappointed, or afraid]. Though our outer self is [progressively] wasting away, yet our inner self is being [progressively] renewed day by day. For our momentary, light distress [this passing trouble] is producing for us an eternal weight of glory [a fullness] beyond all measure [surpassing all comparisons, a transcendent splendor and an endless blessedness]!" (2 Corinthians 4:16-17 AMP)

"My old identity (my old nature) has been co-crucified with Messiah and no longer lives; for the nails of his cross crucified me with him. And now the essence of this new life is no longer mine, for the Anointed One lives his life through me—we live in union as one! My new life is empowered by the faith of the Son of God who loves me so much that he gave himself for me, and dispenses his life into mine!" (Galatians 2:20 TPT, 2017)

"For you were included in the death of Christ and have died with him to the religious system and powers of this world. Don't retreat back to being bullied by the standards and opinions of religion—" (Colossians 2:20 TPT, 2017)

"Sharing in his death by our baptism means that we were co-buried and entombed with him, so that when the Father's glory raised Christ from the dead, we were also raised with him. We have been co-resurrected with him so that we could be empowered to walk in the freshness of new life." (Romans 6:4 TPT, 2017)

"Therefore, if anyone is in Christ, the new creation has come: The old has gone, the new is here!" (2 Corinthians 5:17 NIV)

"Now, if anyone is enfolded into Christ, he has become an entirely new creation. All that is related to the old order has vanished. Behold, everything is fresh and new." (2 Corinthians 5:17 TPT, 2017)

We are a new creation in Christ Jesus, and we have His holy and perfect nature. That's a critical part of walking in our restored identity—walking in the understanding that we are not a sinner saved by grace but in fact a saint. This is a critical part of pursuing freedom from a place of identity. Do you realize that when Jesus died on the cross for us and forgave all our sins, our sins were all in the future? None of them had happened yet. And He still found us worthy to die for! He would do it again and again! But He doesn't have to. It is done. And we are forgiven, redeemed, and a brand-new creation.

You Are a Triune Being
We are spiritual beings. We are a spirit, we have a soul, and we live in a body. We are triune beings just like God Himself is. Our spirit came from God. It's the breath of life that God breathed on us in the very beginning.

Our soul includes our thoughts, feelings, emotions, and desires.

And our body is the biological structure that houses everything, and through which we experience this life here on earth. Our body includes our organs as well as our senses: vision, hearing, touching, smell, and taste. So we are biological, emotional, spiritual, and social beings.

This means that while we live in our earthly body, our biological and emotional being affect who we are spiritually and emotionally, and vice versa. All three parts are connected. None of the three parts is ever isolated. We often tend to treat things as isolated problems. Soul problems, like mental health and emotional issues. Physical problems, like headaches or health challenges. And spiritual problems, like demonic attacks. We need to ask God for discernment when it comes to our holistic being, and with that, we can begin to understand where the root of the problem is, so we can treat it properly and bring freedom from the problem, and not just relief from the symptoms.

The spirit has already been made new. As we discussed, we just need to continually strengthen it by building a daily relationship with Jesus. The body will one day return to dust; we just have to take good care of it while we're here on this earth, by eating well, sleeping well, and exercising. Now, our mind, emotions, and will—meaning our soul—is what needs to be renewed daily. This is the renewal of our mind the Bible talks about in Romans 12:2, as we talked about earlier. Our struggle on this earth is real, and so is sin and evil. The struggle will continue until Jesus comes back. However, the struggle, the sin, and the evil are not in us. They are *against* us. You aren't fighting against flesh and blood, and that includes your own flesh and blood. The battle is against principalities and dark forces of this world, as Paul described in Ephesians 6:12.

When we read about our subconscious, I believe we all understood that we are who we believe we are. Therefore, we must come into agreement and alignment with who God says we are and with His desires for us—perfect health, healing, and restoration. Not only in our spirit but in our body and soul as well—all our thoughts, feelings, emotions, and desires. If we believe any different, we must make a conscious effort to renew our minds about it and upgrade our programming.

As we stand in our identity as children of God, I pray that He will continue to reveal to us who we are in Him and how precious we are to Him.

Activation

In this activation, I would love for you to experience the exchange of natures that took place when you said yes to Jesus. I believe this is an invitation directly from the Holy Spirit to you for an intimate encounter with Him.

I'll describe a scenario to you, so you can align your mind with the Holy Spirit and allow Him to take you and your sanctified imagination wherever He will. Be sure to journal your experience, and have fun capturing every detail!

> You are with Jesus. There is no one else.
> Where are you? What is around you?
> You walk into a space, and you find yourself in front of a huge mirror.
> He asks you to look at yourself and observe. What do you see?
> Is there anything you are very happy with?
> Can you see past physical appearance?
> Is there anything you really dislike? Is it past the physical?
> He asks if there's anything you would like Him to cleanse you from.
> He then exchanges His heart for yours, His nature for yours. He takes yours and gives you His. What does that feel like? What does it look like? What do you feel during and after the exchange?
> Before you leave that space, He faces you, looks into your eyes, and tells you He has a gift for you. What is that gift?

Thank you, Holy Spirit, for beautiful encounters. Thank you, Jesus, for your beautiful gifts. In your name, we praise you and thank you!

Ten

You Are Free to Be Salt and Light

*"Greatness is humility
that doesn't need to be noticed."*
(Source unknown)

I believe there is much false humility in the church today, and a twisted sense of honor, and this has invited idolatry and division into many ministries.

Not long ago, our church was going through a season of change and upgrading our visual image. I believe that upgrade of the physical look reflected and illustrated a new season that God was getting us ready for in the spirit. A few months prior to the launch of this new look, I had a vision in which God showed me a new season coming for the church, particularly for my pastors' lives. Of course, they're the leaders of the ministry; it must come to them and through them first. That makes perfect sense. Little did I know that the launch of this new look was coming. Of course, I knew there's a new season coming, there's obviously preparation from all departments involved, and every department leader is aware. I just didn't know about the visual part. My pastor's wife had mentioned something about visual identity, but I had no idea what she was talking about.

One day, the pastors announced to the leadership team—including me—that we would launch the new visual identity the following weekend. That weekend, they played a video introducing the new visual identity of the church, with the mission and vision, which hadn't changed, and they introduced the new logo. The video was a collection of images, and the pastor narrated in the background. At the end, it all came together with the logo. I was fascinated. I was flabbergasted at the fact that the entire thing illustrated my vision from six months prior. I was weeping from beginning to end. The video was beyond wonderful, the logo stunning, and the fact that it illustrated my vision was incredible.

But truly, what got me weeping was the excellence and greatness and absolute humility in my pastor's wife and her servant's heart. How much work had she dedicated to all of this, with the help of one of our members, who's also great, and both did this on their own, without asking for help, out of a pure heart to serve the congregation. She had a marketing firm create the logo, but she did all the legwork—she and this other member. And this vision and this season was for her before anyone else, and I'm not even sure she realized it. Yet she was the one serving everyone in humility, without the need to be noticed or recognized.

This woman has a full-time job, a husband, and a home. And here she is, serving tirelessly without the need to be noticed. I knew it was her because I know her touch. But no one else did. Afterward, the pastor recognized her as well as the person who had helped her with such excellence. But honestly, she didn't need that recognition. The pastor just loves to give honor where honor is due. She was simply doing what she does, and she does it all the time. She *serves* with excellence the people God has entrusted into her care, and she is great. Because greatness is humility that doesn't need to be noticed. She was being salt, and she was being light, as she always is.

She inspires people around her, and moves them to want to do the same, to be excellent in the way they were called to serve, and to be light and salt. Because in our own ways, we all are called to be salt and light:

> "You are the salt of the earth, but if salt has lost its taste, how shall its saltiness be restored? It is no longer good for anything except to be thrown out and trampled under people's feet. You are the light of the world. A city set on a hill cannot be hidden. Nor do people light a lamp and put it under a basket, but on a stand, and it gives light to all in the house. In the same way, let your light shine before others, so that they may see your

good works and give glory to your Father who is in heaven." (Matthew 5:13-16 ESV)

Let's talk about the salt first. Most people use salt for cooking; food can be tasteless without it. I'm originally from Brazil, and we love to eat white rice pretty much with every meal. Suppose you're making white rice. It looks delicious, it smells delicious, the smell of the cooking garlic permeates the entire home, and you cannot wait to eat it. You're hungry, your steak is ready, and you're waiting for the rice. The rice cooker beeps, and it's ready! When you taste it, you realize you forgot to add salt. Oh no! It tastes like nothing! That is how essential salt is. It enhances and brings out the flavor of the food you're cooking.

However, when you add salt, and it's great and savory and delicious, no one ever says, "Wow, this salt is fantastic!" No, everyone says, "This rice is delicious." And if you added sugar instead of salt, would it be the same? No. Because the taste that salt brings is unique. Only salt can accomplish it.

Although salt is uniquely essential for enhancing the taste of each uniquely delicious food, it's the food that gets the credit for being good, not the salt. However, we all know that without salt, food couldn't reach its full savory potential.

This is a metaphor, and it's talking about us. We are the salt of the earth. God has entrusted people to our circle of influence that we must flavor. They won't reach their potential without our greatness, input, and influence in their lives. This by no means is so that we can boast. This is all because of Jesus in us. It's humility that doesn't need to be noticed. That's why it's important to understand that the salt—us—will not get the credit for it. Because it's not about us. I love how my pastor's wife has been such a beautiful example of this for me and for our church.

In Matthew 5:13, Jesus says that if the salt loses its saltiness, it loses its ability to do what it's supposed to do. Do you know how salt can lose its saltiness? I found this to be profound. And of course Jesus has a message for us here, as He always does. Salt loses its saltiness by contamination or by separation. Can you just see how profound that is? We can lose our ability to do what God has called us to do when the impurities of this world contaminate our hearts. Our hearts can be contaminated by thinking we should be getting credit for all that we're doing. Pride—or false humility, which is pride in disguise—is one of the greatest contaminators.

We can also lose saltiness when we're contaminated by our own greatness without humility. It can sound like this: "Surely someone besides me could have done all the hard work for this; I'm the leader." Or, "I should not be carrying all this weight on my own; I'm the leader, and I have enough spiritual weight already." Or, "I'm not being honored; they don't honor me the way they should." Or, "Why do I need to do all this by myself? Aren't there others in the church capable of helping?" There are so many factors that could contaminate us. Sometimes, these thoughts are planted by other people who think they're honoring the leader. But in reality, they're bringing division to the ministry and contamination to the heart of the leader. I won't get into any more examples now. I'll leave you with plenty of room for the Holy Spirit to move and reveal to you if there's anything contaminating you and removing your saltiness.

The second thing that can get us to lose our saltiness is separation. Nothing can separate us from God's love, but some things can surely separate us from our awareness of His love for us. And that could be sin, mistakes we make, which the enemy uses to accuse us and say that we're far from God. This is obviously impossible, because He is in us. But somehow, we end up believing that lie. Or even separate ourselves from other believers. Isolation. A lonely sheep is easier to become prey, and so is a lonely believer.

I encourage you to spend some time with the Holy Spirit and ask God to check your heart to see if there's a separation that needs to be addressed. Sometimes, the easiest thing to do when we're in a place of emotional hardship is to separate ourselves from other believers. We tend to think and believe that no one understands us. Of course, there are some places that are absolutely not healthy to be in. But the Word of God says that iron sharpens iron (Proverbs 27:17), and that it's not suitable for man to be alone—referring to humankind, not gender (Genesis 2:8). Therefore, the more we isolate ourselves, the more likely we'll immerse ourselves into a pool of self-pity due to separation.

Isn't it amazing the correlation that Jesus makes between salt and us, and how salt can lose its saltiness? I found it to be profound. The difference is that, unlike regular salt, we have been restored. He has paid a price to redeem our "saltiness," our purpose, and our greatness.

So if He is bringing anything to the surface for you, it's because you're ready to be healed and to receive complete restoration.

Now the light. Think of times when you've watched a stage play. Have you noticed how beautiful the spotlight makes people look? We know they're important because they have the spotlight on them. No one says, "That light is great." Everyone notices the person under the light. However, if the light wasn't there, you couldn't see the show at all. The light is essential to make the person under the light shine, but the person gets the credit, not the light.

The concept is the same for us. Jesus says we are the light. We are the salt. He is saying that we're *essential*. We're the ones who make a difference everywhere we go. We're the ones bringing flavor out of the people around us. He has placed us where we are for such a time as this. When we enter a place of darkness, we light it up because light is superior to darkness. He has chosen us to collaborate and partner with Him to make this world a better place. We matter!

We're supposed to make a difference in the life of those around us, without expecting any credit for doing so. Salt and light empower. They get little or no credit, and yet without it, nothing would be the same.

That's who we are. Salt and light. Essential for the lives of all those God has entrusted us with—friends, spouses, children, employees. We're essential for their lives, their growth, and their well-being. Who we are in Christ is essential for their lives. In the same way, who they are in Christ is essential for our lives. And that's why God brought us together. Christ in us, believers, is the hope of glory!

Let's not underestimate that. Let's be salt and light, by serving others with excellence and greatness, in humility and kindness, without expecting credit for it. This is powerful and life-changing. When we have the humility to empower others as salt empowers food and as light illumines the person, expecting no credit in return and without the need to be noticed, we enter a whole new level of freedom. I believe something great happens at this level that words cannot express. It's a divine reward. A deep satisfaction that can be given only by our heavenly Father to those who are free to be salt and light.

Activation

This activation may get you a little outside your comfort zone, as activations usually do, in a good way! If you aren't sure how you're called to serve, this may be a two-part activation for you and even more outside your comfort zone, and that's okay.

Let's look for someone we can serve outside the circle of people we usually serve, and serve that person in the way we believe God has called us to serve. This could be delivering a word of encouragement to a person at the grocery store. Or praying for a stranger at a bus stop. Or doing the nails of an elderly person at a nursing home. Or cleaning someone's bathroom. Or it may be simply giving someone a big hug.

How has God called you to serve? If you don't know, just ask Him. You may get an inclination in your heart, or it may be something you naturally love to do. You can go with that for now and continue to lean into the Holy Spirit as He continues to reveal to you how He has called you to be salt and light. The idea here is not to put pressure on yourself at all, but to experience the next level of serving with humility, without expecting anything in return, and without the need to be noticed.

Eleven

You Are Free to Be You— And Not Compare Yourself

"Comparison is the thief of joy."
Theodore Roosevelt

I first heard that quote from someone, and I didn't know it was a quote originally from Theodore Roosevelt, the youngest person ever to assume the presidency of our country, the United States of America. This leads me to believe that he was a wise man who understood the importance of not comparing himself to anyone else.

We may be super happy about a new pair of shoes until someone shows up with their new pair of exotic, crocodile-skin, luxurious, high-end shoes. It kills our joy because now we've compared our shoes to others that seem better than ours. The same is true with our gifts, talents, skills, abilities, and even anointing.

Comparison is different from envy, but I believe it precedes it. And it turns into envy if we don't become aware of it and deal with it wisely before it becomes a greater monster.

When I was a kid, my best friend and I wanted to make some cash, so we decided to make some sweets to sell in school. I would make chocolate lollipops, and she would make this Brazilian-Italian sweet that she knew how to make, which was incredibly delicious. I made tons of lollipops, and I was so excited for her to come so I could show her. When she came with a tray of her mouthwatering sweets, she asked me to try one, and of course, they were delicious—but my joy was killed. Why? I couldn't understand it. I truly couldn't wrap my mind around it as a child. But later in life, I surely did. It was because I compared my sweet-making skills to hers. I couldn't make the sweets she did. All I could do was melt chocolate, put it in the plastic shapes with a stick, and make lollipops. But her sweets were divine. So I compared my sweet-making skills to hers, although as a kid I didn't even realize that's what I was doing.

That comparison killed my joy. It didn't matter that I'd made a hundred lollipops, or how happy I was prior to her arrival with her heavenly sweets, or how excited I was to sell all of it the next day. That joy-killer made me sabotage our little business, and soon we weren't doing it anymore. My friend was sad, and so was I, and we didn't even understand why. We were just kids. But there it was—comparison, the killer of joy and a major saboteur.

I wish I could tell you that this was the only encounter I had with comparison. Unfortunately, it was not. Comparison followed me well into my teenage years. I've always had everything I needed, wanted, and more, but when we compare ourselves to others, we always fall short, and we end up sabotaging our own joy. I did that for so long and never even realized I was doing it.

To be honest, I don't think my lack of realization was due to the fact that I was young or that I wasn't yet walking with the Lord. I see believers who are walking with the Lord and who are fully grown adults having the same behavior. I just think we don't know what we don't know.

It wasn't until the end of my twenties that I realized that I was living the comparison game. And this is how I realized it. I was a manager at a company, and a new believer. One day, I had an argument with another manager at work about something related to sales. A sales environment can be hostile, and that was my life. Her behavior and attitude toward me opened my eyes to how I'd been acting toward her, and how it promoted unhealthy competition and comparison. As my eyes were opened to my own attitude at that moment, I was able to see how I'd been comparing myself overall, at different levels, in different areas of my life.

Has that ever happened to you? Suddenly you have an epiphany, and your eyes are open to something that has been there all along, and you hadn't seen. It was like I stepped out of my own self and I could watch my life as in a movie—and my behavior was not nice. It was not kind. And comparison was causing most of it. This little movie took me back all the way to my chocolate lollipop-making days. I suddenly had a realization of what was sabotaging my joy, that familiar yet unidentified saboteur—comparison.

From that day forward, I was so aware of this saboteur and killer of joy. And I was no longer willing to let it sabotage me or kill my joy. It didn't mean it would never try to come against me again. But I was aware of it, and I could recognize it. Every time it came against me, it had less and less power, because I became better and better in my counterattack. When I say counterattack, I mean against the enemy—the killer of joy, comparison—and not against people.

Our counterattack is owning our own identity. Owning our own gifts, talents, qualities, and the good about ourselves, which sometimes we have a hard time seeing. We learn to recognize them and grow in them. We let go of false humility, knowing that God gave us things that make us special and unique. Because true humility isn't thinking less of ourselves, as we often tend to do. It is thinking of ourselves less.

The more we get to know ourselves, the less we want to compare ourselves with someone else, and the more we can appreciate others for who they are. Because at the end of the day, God designed us all to complete and complement each other—not compete or compare.

Don't think that I share these stories with you because I enjoy exposing my past flaws. I don't. I share them because I want you to know that overcoming our past flaws is part of our pursuit of a lifestyle of freedom. Every time we overcome something that comes against us or tries to keep us in bondage, we conquer another level of freedom in that area, and in this manner, we grow from glory to glory and from freedom to freedom.

We'll be growing until we see Jesus face to face. There's always more glory and more freedom. We aren't done. By sharing our past flaws, and the testimonies of what we've been able to overcome with the Holy Spirit, we're creating an atmosphere for Him to do it again, and we're inviting others into the areas of freedom that we've already conquered.

As beautiful and unique as we are, God made us to help others shine as well. We couldn't possibly do that without recognizing our own self-worth. We aren't here to compare ourselves to others. It's okay to be inspired and motivated by the way others carry themselves and the Holy Spirit in them, but never okay to compare. Because no matter how hard we try, we'll always make a poor and lousy version of the other person we're trying to be.

As we continue to pursue freedom from a place of identity, it's important to know and understand that God thought about us profoundly before the creation of the earth. He created us so uniquely, and it's essential to embrace our uniqueness. We're free to be who God created us to be without comparison. May we discover who that is.

Activation

Take some time with the Holy Spirit and ask Him to reveal to you some of your unique characteristics that He loves about you. What are some features about your character that resemble the character of God? You were created in His image.

Ask a few people you love and trust what are some qualities that are unique about you, and what are some qualities that they love about you.

Now ask yourself what qualities are unique about yourself, and what qualities you love about yourself.

Ask the Holy Spirit if there's any area in which you've been comparing yourself with others, and take some time to listen. If there is, ask God to forgive you, accept His forgiveness, and receive the fullness of who you are. You are free to be you.

Take some time to journal and meditate on this. This is important!

Twelve

You Are Free to Multiply

*"Gifts are free,
but maturity is expensive."*
Bill Johnson, *Spiritual Java*

A few years ago, my sister bought a farmhouse. It has a good piece of land, enough that she could have some fruit trees, which she always wanted, and you can't really have that in the small, prefabricated backyards we get in most homes in the heart of Miami. She was excited, and she was planning on all the fruit trees she would get.

One day, I went to a website to buy a baby fruit tree as a birthday gift for her—I know, odd birthday gift, but that's what she wanted. I discovered that fruit trees were actually quite expensive. She and I started talking about it sometime later, as I was wondering why she couldn't just plant the seeds from the fruit we ate. We already bought the fruit; the seeds came with it. They were a plus. It made sense to me.

She explained to me that a process needed to happen for that seed to become a baby tree. And that process required a lot of love, tender care and attention, special care and special plant food that was designed particularly for the type of plant, and whatever else it needed—I can't recall everything she mentioned. Now it made sense why people would charge so much money for the baby trees. It was really the process they were billing people for. No wonder they call the places that sell baby trees nurseries.

The point is that every fruit has seeds, and the seed contains the potential to become like the fruit that it came from. However, to become that fruit, it takes time, care, nurturing, the right environment and atmosphere, the right amount of sunlight, nutrients, and whatever else the process may require. The seed is a gift that comes with the fruit when we buy the fruit from somewhere or someone. The fruit is maturity. Gifts are free, but maturity is expensive. That's why the more mature the tree is, when we buy it, the more expensive it is.

By this time, we understand that we all have been given, for free, the gift of freedom. And it was given to us as a seed. It's now our responsibility to pursue a lifestyle of freedom—to mature, to multiply that freedom to all areas of our life, to live it out, to grow it, and to turn it into fruit.

Just as a fruit has seeds that can multiply that fruit, *we* are God's seed. We have His DNA. Therefore, we have a responsibility to multiply. To mature and to become like the One we were made after.

> "And God said, 'Let the earth sprout vegetation, plants yielding seed, and fruit trees bearing fruit in which is their seed, each according to its kind, on the earth.' And it was so." (Genesis 1:11 ESV)

When God created us, He planted His seed in us. He created the potential for us to be everything He intended us to be. He created our identity to be like the Creator Himself. He gave us His DNA.

> "Then God said, 'Let us make man in our image, after our likeness.'" (Genesis 1:26 ESV)

> "Then the LORD God formed a man from the dust of the ground and breathed into his nostrils the breath of life, and the man became a living being." (Genesis 2:7 NIV)

Back in the beginning, as soon as God created humankind, He blessed us and said: Be fruitful and multiply, and subdue the earth. This reveals our purpose. Or at least the beginning of our purpose. To multiply! Multiply His character, multiply His glory, multiply the gifts and talents that He has placed in each of us. And *subdue*—have dominion over the earth. This requires maturity. It requires that we continually pursue the gift of freedom that we inherited, and that we multiply it from a place of identity.

What does this mean to us? How do we do that? How do we multiply and mature? We have seen and understood how God planted a seed in us that is, in essence, the potential to be like Him. So to be fruitful is to make sure we cultivate that seed in us, the fruit of the Spirit, so that we become more and more like Him. We multiply the character and glory of God by walking in "love [unselfish concern for others], joy, [inner] peace, patience [not the ability to wait, but how we act while waiting], kindness, goodness, faithfulness, gentleness, and self-control." (Galatians 5:22-23 AMP)

You don't have to beg and cry for an orange tree to produce oranges. It's just what it does. But as we learned earlier, we do need to provide adequate conditions for the tree to grow and mature and give fruit. If we don't provide the young tree what it needs, such as nutrients, sun exposure, and good soil, it won't produce fruit, although it has the potential to do so. The same goes for us. We shouldn't have to beg and cry to be free and produce the fruit of the Spirit. We are already free, and the fruit of the Spirit is already in us—it's who we are already. What we have to do is provide adequate conditions. The right exposure to the Son (Jesus), the right amount of water (the Holy Spirit), and good soil (a tender heart, plowed by the love of the Father).

The fruit of the Spirit that we produce when we cultivate the Holy Spirit in us is the multiplication of God's character—His goodness and glory. Unlike everything else that God created, He created us in a unique way. We're the only living creature that He breathed on. The word *breath* in that verse we read can also mean spirit. He breathed His Spirit into us as He created us in His image.

We have within us the Spirit of the living God, His seed, and His DNA, and we're free to multiply it as we continue our journey, pursuing freedom from a place of identity.

Activation

This is your last activation for this book. So we made it one that you can multiply!

We multiply the character and glory of God by walking in "love [unselfish concern for others], joy, [inner] peace, patience [not the ability to wait, but how we act while waiting], kindness, goodness, faithfulness, gentleness, and self-control" (Galatians 5:22-23 AMP).

Ask the Holy Spirit which part of this "fruit" you should focus on. Choose one. Each morning as you wake up, say, "Good morning, Holy Spirit," and ask Him to please help you keep your focus this day on the attribute you chose from Galatians 5:22-23. Ask Him to bring this to your mind throughout the day.

You can do this for as many days as you feel called to, and you can move back and forth between the different parts of the "fruit" as you feel the Holy Spirit leading you. Observe throughout your day how you were able to exercise your godly character.

As always, I suggest you journal.

Closing Comments on the Pursuit of Freedom

*"I press on to reach the end of the race
and receive the heavenly prize for which God,
through Christ Jesus, is calling us."*
Philippians 3:14 NLT

We all deal with limiting beliefs that in some way keep us from experiencing the fullness of the freedom that Jesus died for us to have. But we've learned that we have access to a higher reality through Jesus, and we've journeyed together through three steps that have equipped and empowered us to continually pursue the lifestyle of freedom that gives us access to that reality daily—and, most importantly, honors the sacrifice of our Savior.

We started with the understanding of what freedom is and what it isn't. I'm sure you were blown away by some revelations you had of simple things you defined as freedom in your subconscious, and suddenly you discovered that these were incorrectly defined. Not to mention all the emotional crises that we sometimes go through, and it turns out we were breaking free and learning to get deeper into our own pursuit and relationship with God. That describes some of the hard years for me. Were you able to identify some crisis in your life that led you into deeper freedom? I'm cheering you on! I encourage you to journal and take notes. (Perhaps you will write the next book New Life publishes. You never know!)

Next, we understood some basic steps in pursuing a lifestyle of freedom from a place of victory and identity in Christ. We aren't victims, and we aren't sinners. We are more than conquerors.

I pray that in each chapter, you were empowered by the activations, and that through them, your connection with the Holy Spirit increased, your relationship with Jesus was strengthened, and the love of the Father in you grew even greater.

So the big question is: How do you know you are freer? How do you know that your mind is being renewed, and that you are in fact adopting new mindsets?

Well, throughout my own journey and my experience in walking others through their personal journey, I've been able to observe some tangible signs that are a result of deeper freedom and a renewed mindset. Perhaps observing these signs in your own life will help you determine the efforts of your pursuit. Keep in mind that these are signs to observe, not a checklist. These are results that come automatically from your pursuit of freedom through a genuine relationship with Christ. These aren't the things you need to be pursuing.

- The way you see situations changes. You begin to see things from a place of gratitude and trust.
- The meditation of your heart changes (the things you think about). You'll catch yourself meditating on the Word more often.
- The way you speak changes. You begin to have a language that's filled with hope and faith.
- Your attitude toward others changes. You begin to trust people and their intentions toward you.
- Your attitude toward circumstances changes. You begin to have positive expectations for the outcome of things.
- Your attitude toward yourself changes. You grow in self-love and self-respect. You begin to appreciate even your weaknesses, because you know God will show up, and it will be an opportunity not only for Him to show off but also for you to grow.

I know that a new level of freedom has been unlocked in your spirit. And what's next? More! There's always more! Nothing limits you, now that you've been activated to pursue a lifestyle of freedom and live a higher reality on earth as it is in heaven.

Here are just some tips that you may find helpful to continue embracing this process:

Give yourself a break. Don't be too tough on yourself, if you find yourself going back into old habits and mindsets. At the same time, embrace the process and the discomfort. Hold yourself accountable and have accountability partners.

Submit to your pastoral leadership, even if you don't fully agree with them. Submission doesn't always mean agreement.

Bring yourself back into the process of freedom, bring yourself back into the truth, the Word of God, and be aware of triggers that could make you want to fall back into habits that keep you enslaved and avoid them.

Do not be ashamed of getting help if you need to. Therapy, counseling, whatever it is you may need, even if it's as simple as hiring help to remove some of the load from your plate. It's okay. You don't have to be Wonder Woman or Superman. They don't exist. They're a cartoon. You just have to be *you*, fully alive.

Heal the root of any harmful thought patterns and habits. You can use the tools I share in this book, including the practical Freedom Technique that my friend shared with us, and it will help set you free from all belief systems and thoughts that may keep you from walking in freedom.

I know it's hard to feel pain, and no one likes to. I sure don't. But sometimes, it's necessary to allow the pain to be felt and to acknowledge that it's there, so God can heal it. Don't try to shut it down, don't try to numb it, don't try to mute it. Allow yourself to feel the pain if the pain is there. Cry, scream, and allow the ugly snot to come out of your nose if it has to. Get it all out. Then allow the Holy Spirit, the ultimate comforter and healer, to comfort and heal you.

Once that's all done, fix your crown on your head, hold Jesus's hands really tight, put yourself back together, and keep going—because there's always more waiting for you! And it's going to be marvelous!

With all my love,
Tassyane

Step IV

FREEDOM TECHNIQUE

Step IV is all about the Freedom Technique developed by my friend, and certified cognitive behavioral therapist Michelle Gonçalves, to help her patients walk in freedom. This technique is surely part of the pursuit of a lifestyle of freedom.

Disclosure: Please know that this is a technique. This is not a miracle or by any means a replacement for any current treatment that you may be using or medications you may be taking. By no means are we suggesting that you stop anything without consulting a doctor or without the consent of the professional help you're currently seeing. Neither is it a formula. Ask God how you can personalize it for your best outcome.

Thirteen

Introduction to the Freedom Technique and Its Founder

Michelle Gonçalves specializes in helping her patients improve their quality of life by providing tools for self-evaluation of different aspects of their lives—social, emotional, mental, cognitive, and behavioral.

Michelle provides a psychoanalytical and behavioral line in her psychotherapeutic sessions. Her service has many facets and dynamics, and her clients benefit from her cheerful and welcoming personality. She becomes a mix of a partner, mother, fan, therapist, and friend in terms of the therapeutic process applied to each of her patients individually. For her, it's essential that everyone feels welcomed, understood, supported, challenged, and helped. Her work aims to promote and facilitate the construction of everyone's best version of life and dreams, according to their own purpose.

In this process, she unmasks limiting perceptions and beliefs, helping her patients voice known or unknown trauma, and promoting healing. She challenges their existing perspectives, driving them to change, to align directions, and to balance their life priorities. All this by promoting tools to live a free, abundant, and victorious life.

She's a mother of four amazing girls, with her husband of almost thirty years, Alexandre. They've been together since they were kids. They've been through thick and thin, and they come out better and stronger together on the other side of whatever mountain and giant they may face.

Resilient is fitting description for her, but not quite enough to describe how I see Michelle. She's strong and courageous and fights with grit, endurance, and perseverance for what she believes is right. Michelle is a commendable woman with a beautiful heart and a true, genuine desire to live in freedom and to help others do the same. She has a passion for souls, a desire for Jesus's pure and true love to reign in every area of humanity. Needless to say, I love her wholeheartedly and admire who she is.

Michelle originally came up with this technique as she researched ways to renew her own mind, to bring herself to a better place and to grow and evolve. This became a tool that she uses in her therapy sessions to help bring healing and freedom to many of her patients. I appreciate her desire to always be growing, and her generosity to share that growth with the world around her.

In the next section, I'll share part of the initial conversation Michelle and I had when she first introduced this technique to me, and I'll paraphrase her words in my own words, according to how I understood them and what I took from it. Then I'll share the application, including some of my thoughts from the time she invited me into the process of writing it.

The next chapter is on the acronym of freedom and the instructions she developed for each letter. Finally, the last chapter of this section includes a couple of examples that she provided from patients (while protecting their identity). The scenarios are accurate to provide you with real-life examples, but their names and details were changed for privacy.

Fourteen

What Is the Freedom Technique?

The Freedom Technique challenges and unravels our limiting perceptions and hidden mental prisons that cause us so much difficulty in dealing with our own lives, relationships, directions, and results in life. This technique will teach our minds to look in the right direction, guiding each step toward achieving the right goals, making new and more accurate choices, and achieving more positive results.

With the mind positioned in a wise, centered state and with the choices and results aligned with our heart's desires and the reality of our lives, this Freedom Technique will open doors for us to experience the feeling of growth, transformation, and true freedom. We'll gain in freedom of choice and permission to be our best selves, which were previously imprisoned by our limiting genetics, perceptions, and emotions. With this technique, we'll have a transformed vision of ourselves, our history, and the people around us, leading to transformed actions and behaviors.

This technique consists of daily steps to reveal prisons in our minds caused by extremely powerful emotional memories creating lenses and wrong perspectives. We'll learn daily steps for breaking those emotional patterns and developing a new perspective based on truth. We'll learn about rebuilding our foundation from the ground up, destroying strongholds, and discovering who we really are and what our purpose in life is—then walking in that identity and purpose and changing our destiny to match what has been predestined for us from the foundation of the earth, victory.

"By changing perspectives with the real truth and applying new behaviors," Michelle Gonçalves tells us, "you will change the structure of your memories, and after repetition, it will cause a change in the brain structure too."

The only real truth is the Word of God. The Word of God is powerful. It has enough power to change a shapeless blob into planet earth, so it must be able to change our thinking and restructure our brains as well.

Michelle believes that following the steps of this technique daily, and reaching our own daily goals, will allow us to engage with our mind and live out our highest calling. She believes that the ultimate result of this daily soul-and-spirit engagement will be the renewal of our own minds to see what's already available and to access the victories that are already ours, made possible through the sacrifice and love of Jesus.

By promoting awareness through the Freedom Technique, we can understand our difficulties, analyze our perceptions, emotions, choices, and beliefs, and externalize them. We bring to consciousness hidden emotions from the subconscious caused by trauma. When memories cause a lot of pain, the brain keeps them in the unconscious so as not to cause more emotional damage than we can bear. By bringing awareness to these memories, we can consciously heal, gain self-responsibility, align perceptions, and make choices that will be more beneficial to ourselves versus the ones that kept us captive to a mindset of slavery. All without the influence of trauma.

Through the technique, we also sharpen cognitive and behavioral aspects bringing memories, thoughts, emotions, and behaviors to be revealed and evaluated. Through changing behaviors, we can experience new results. And by maintaining the consistency of practice in repetition, we'll create new neuronal synapses, paths, memories, and directions by putting new neuroplasticity into practice.

Michelle recommends a minimum of ninety days of practicing the technique to see permanent changes.

Let's look at the steps to understand better how it can be applied.

Fifteen

Freedom Technique in Action

Each letter of the acronym FREEDOM has a meaning, and it represents a step of its own within the technique.
Fact
Revealing
Encountering
Enlightening
Dedicating
On action
Mindfulness

Fact
What is the fact in question, and what is the difficulty being experienced?

In this step, you'll report or write down the fact and the difficulty you're facing. What do you need freedom from? At this point, you aren't trying to get to feelings and thoughts yet, just facts.

Here's an example: "I'm often rude to my children. That's a fact I need freedom from. I don't need to be rude to my thirteen-year-old son because he forgot to put his socks in the laundry basket. There are better ways to communicate, even if I've already asked him to do this a million times."

Capture the facts. Write them down.

Revealing
Reveal the feelings and thoughts about the fact.

In this step, you reveal the whole story. What are the feelings, thoughts, and perceptions you're experiencing about this fact, and who is involved in the situation? Write down why you think you're living this situation.

Dig deeper for the thoughts, feelings, or emotions behind the fact. What is taking over your mind or your peace? Facts don't take over; thoughts, feelings, and emotions behind the facts do. When you saw those socks, how did you feel? What went through your mind? Did you feel frustrated? Why? Did you feel as if your work around the house is insignificant? Did you feel unappreciated? Did you feel unheard because you've expressed your desire for the socks to go into the laundry basket so many times, yet it hasn't happened? Ask yourself some additional questions related to your fact. Invite the Holy Spirit to give you all the right questions and get it all down on paper.

Capture your thoughts and feelings to the best of your ability. It doesn't have to be perfect, it doesn't have to be logical, nor does it have to make sense. This is like a brain dump where you begin to get out everything that's in your mind. Whatever way it comes out is perfectly fine.

Encountering

It's time to encounter all the experiences that led to these feelings, thoughts, and perceptions.

In this step, you'll find answers for limiting beliefs that you learned and archived throughout your life through difficult or traumatizing experiences within your family, in the society you live in, or in relationships and experiences overall.

Think, pray, and ask the Holy Spirit for revelation now. This is the time to encounter limiting beliefs. What do you believe is leading you to feel or think the way you're feeling and thinking? Understanding that will get you out of the hamster wheel. Observing triggers will help you in this process.

Perhaps the socks on the floor made you feel the way you did because you have a limiting belief that you are unworthy, and that's why your own child doesn't listen to you. Perhaps the voice in your head—caused by that limiting belief—is saying, "It's not your work around the house that's insignificant; *you* are insignificant." These are examples of limiting beliefs.

The goal is to encounter the root of why you believe what you do. What exactly is limiting you from moving forward and keeping you in a loop that never ends? Pinpoint that lie or limiting belief that's throwing off your thoughts and emotions. You may have to dig into some childhood memories to discover the root of some belief systems, which can be painful in some cases. Encountering the wrong belief system may take time. Even if you don't remember exactly when and how that belief system was first planted in you, it's important that you identify what's behind the feeling or thought you initially had.

Remember, it took your whole life to build that wrong belief system. Be gracious to yourself now that you're trying to dismantle it, but be firm nonetheless. Dig until you get to the bottom of it. Allow yourself to feel the pain, but don't stay in the pit of pain. Always have intercessors praying for you and with you. Take responsibility, but don't blame yourself. You are not a victim. You have choices and are choosing to improve. That's great!

Enlightening

Enlightenment leads to clarity—what is the desired outcome for the fact?

What mindset would you like to have about the whole thing? What does the light at the end of the tunnel look like for you?

Now that you're fully aware of your limiting belief, it's time to enlighten your mind with truth from the Word of God, to gain ideas and see what the best outcome may be. Clear your perspective for a moment and ask: What does the Word of God say about this?

Keep in mind that you are not a victim of people and circumstances. What happened to you may not have been your fault, but it's your responsibility to move forward, and you're doing just that.

If you looked through the Bible to find verses that talk about your worth, you would come across these verses, among many others:

> "For we are His workmanship [His own master work, a work of art], created in Christ Jesus [reborn from above—spiritually transformed, renewed, ready to be used] for good works, which God prepared [for us] beforehand [taking paths which He set], so that we would walk in them [living the good life which He prearranged and made ready for us]." (Ephesians 2:10 AMP)

"You formed my innermost being, shaping my delicate inside and my intricate outside, and wove them all together in my mother's womb. I thank you, God, for making me so mysteriously complex! Everything you do is marvelously breathtaking. It simply amazes me to think about it! How thoroughly you know me, Lord! You even formed every bone in my body when you created me in the secret place; carefully, skillfully you shaped me from nothing to something. You saw who you created me to be before I became me! Before I'd ever seen the light of day, the number of days you planned for me were already recorded in your book." (Psalm 139:13-16 TPT, 2017)

How amazing are God's thoughts regarding your significance and worth, that He would take the time to record those thoughts in the Book of Life!

Can you see how this begins to shift your perspective? For instance, you can now use these verses to replace the limiting belief of unworthiness.

Make note of who you want to be, what your goal is, and by when. For example: "I want to be heard by my children, so I'll be a better communicator by the end of the year." In this way, you can begin to seek the help you need to be a better communicator. What does that look like? Is it a therapist? Is it a communication class? Is it more conversations? Does your son also need help?

Can you see how this unfolds a process that has action items that will move you forward? That's what happens when you enlighten. You can see things from a bigger picture. It's not action time yet; you're just taking notes.

Dedicating

Dedication is the time to focus on your desired results and not on feelings.

Understand what thoughts and feelings are aligned with the truth so that you can look, feel, and act toward what you want to build going forward, in order to achieve your desired outcome. Rewrite your story, even if you don't think or feel this way yet. Begin to recreate and restructure thought patterns and neuro-psychological interactions to have new attitudes, and soon you'll start to see things from a perspective of triumph that will help free you daily from limitations that previously paralyzed you.

It's the repetition of this process that creates change. What do you believe you must change and do to win this victory? What are the steps? What's stopping you from achieving it? What do you need to do first? What needs to happen?

Consider what your choices are, then prioritize. What changes need to happen? What positions and actions do you have to take? Which tools do you need? What's the first step? What's your motivation?

Ask God. Listen. Write it down.

Now that you have a fresh perspective and a plan of action, take a moment to take ownership of this perspective change. This is important, and this is a daily step you need to take moving forward. It takes twenty-one days to build a new habit and ninety days to build a new lifestyle. But only God knows how long it takes to build a good new stronghold in your mind to replace the old wrong one forever.

On Action

It's time to put it all into action, turning new thoughts into actions to achieve desired new results.

You'll now put into practice the plan you created. You've already begun to analyze it. You know what you want, and you've meditated on it, thought and prayed about it. You know what thoughts, feelings, attitudes, and resources you need to put it into practice and build new results, transforming the story of your fact and the story of your life. Now is time for action.

Start writing down the first possible step that you can take, and then the next, on through until the last in order of priority.

Be realistic. Write down the timeframe in which you will complete each step, from the first to the last. Be specific. Within each step, capture what you'll be doing, the goals and gains of the step, and the estimated completion date. Sign your action plan to give it credibility. Write down the next steps before finishing the previous one to stay motivated. Focus on the goal. Complete each one until your final victory.

This is not by any means an invitation to overwhelm yourself. That's why it's a process, and this step is all the way toward the end of the process. Remember, you're already victorious, and you're already winning in life. You've come a long way already.

Consider these questions:
— Do you need to hire help around the house?
— Can you afford it?
— What can you delegate? And to whom?
— Do you need to have a reward system for the kids that will be attractive so they can have extra motivation for chores?
— What are the chores they can do without you having to redo them?
— Do you need therapy?
— Do the kids need therapy?
— Do you need more quiet time with the Lord every day?

These are practical and actionable items that will help make life easier and will help organize your day and your mind better. Take some time with the Holy Spirit and invite Him to help you determine some actionable items that will help you in your day-to-day life. Be open to changes on a regular basis. Don't write these in stone. As life and schedules change, and as priorities shift, be open!

Mindfulness

Mindfulness. Wise mind. Dealing with the fact in a mature, responsible, and transformed way.

This is where you'll begin reaching new emotional, social, cognitive, and personal structures about the fact and how you see yourself around that fact now, with a new mindset. It's important to keep a journal in this process to write down all your paths and journeys, as well as the victories you achieve.

A few things are imperative to keep in mind at this point:
— You know God and you are more significant than this fact.
— You are living in abundance, balance, and triumph over this fact.
— You've reached your final goal about this particular fact.
— You're moving on to your next journey.

Mindfulness is a state of mind that we should always be in. We should always live mindful of our own thinking. Don't suppose that this is a one-and-done kind of thing, but instead, be vigilant of your mind and your thoughts, and if you notice an intrusive thought, feeling, or emotion, take care of it right away before it takes root in you. A renewed mind is a free mind.

The renewal of the mind is a constant thing while we live on earth. And that's what mindfulness is.

Sixteen

Real-Life Examples

Of course, as mentioned before, the examples have been altered to protect clients' identities, but they're actual examples provided by Michelle to give us an accurate idea of how she uses this technique daily.

Example One
Twenty-five years old, female, multiple anxieties and fears, dissatisfied with professional life.
Main goal: To feel better about myself, reduce anxiety, believe in my dreams, and change my professional field (financial life, transformed self-worth).
First step: Met with the therapist, addressed issues, and made a commitment to self.
What that commitment looked like for the patient:
I'm going to start having a moment with myself; motivate myself daily with positive words and daily devotionals; take care of my appearance; and keep a journal and start writing everything I'm feeling and what I want.
I'm also going to look for people who've achieved similar things that I would like to achieve—to learn from them, be inspired by them, and keep myself motivated, knowing that it's possible to achieve my heart's desire.
The patient signed an agreement with herself and committed to doing these things consistently for twenty-one consecutive days.
Second step: Three weeks after the first step, I'm going to take the second step. I'll begin to research a new career choice. Important bases to consider: areas that match my personality, gifts, talents,

and tastes. Find out the demand for this branch and study the profit margins.

Example Two
Forty-five years old, female, married, mother of three.

Fact: I don't feel valued, loved, or cared for by my husband. I wanted to have a completely different life. I wanted to separate from him, but I can't. Therefore, I'm unhappy and hopeless.

Reveal: I feel like the worst woman in the world, a failure, worthless, unsuccessful, and I don't know why he does so much evil to me. If I agree with him, perfect, he loves me. If not, everything goes downhill. Fights, discussions, and misunderstandings. I give my life for him and my children, I don't take care of or prioritize myself, I work with him, and I hate it when he's there. I feel unrecognized and kicked around. I have dreams, and I don't have the time or motivation to move forward. He also puts dirt on me and everything I do. I'm always involved in his demands, which must be the way he wants, without considering what I think, feel, or want. Living in this manner makes me feel so much hate and sadness that sometimes I would like to die to solve it all. Lots of anxiety and co-dependencies. When he yells or loses his temper and takes his frustration out on the boys and me, I feel like walking away and leaving him. He deserves to be alone. But I can never do it! And then I go back to the frustration of living this miserable life. Sometimes, I think I'm crazy and ungrateful, but that feeling is real inside of me because of my life and the relationship we live. I eat excessively and drink a lot, I'm overweight, and I don't feel beautiful, nor capable, much less attractive.

Encountering: The limiting mentalities I find are that I am incapable, I'm not smart or beautiful, I don't even know how to speak or express myself, I have to perform to be loved. No one sees my value, money is evil, many bad things happen in the world, my life is hell, I deserve to go through these difficulties and sufferings. Everyone has everything, and I have nothing. I don't think I deserve it. I just wanted a family, peace, and a career, but I don't think I can, because my family is a failure, and it's horrible. I am a failure. I see no way out but to separate from my husband. I think he is mean. People are mean to me, and I allow them to do mean things to me, afraid of losing the people in my life. I need to live alone. Nobody understands me. But I'm afraid of being punished by God.

Enlighten: My biggest dream is that I could have a structured family, a partner by my side who doesn't suck so much out of me, who isn't so problematic or negative, and who loves and supports me so I can live my best version. I would love to be free of anxieties and proud of myself and my life. I wish I could have a career, something that I like, that fulfills me, that I identify with. A routine, like any other woman—work, finances, a car, a story, a life, and achievements. And I wish I didn't feel imprisoned by this relationship that slowly consumes and destroys me.

Dedication: Instead of believing that this is my final reality, the reality that my parents lived, I want to restructure my own value, a new story. Instead of staying paralyzed by my limiting perceptions, I will change them.

In a therapy session with Michelle, I decided that the first step would be to change how I see myself—to begin taking care of myself and investing in myself. I can't change anyone nor beg for their love, respect, and priority. However, I can change things in my own life. I will continue being a mother and a wife. I will let everyone deal with their own choices and personal life, and I will take care of mine. I will take care of myself physically, mentally, emotionally, and professionally, because no one has the power to do that for me. After all, I want to position myself to be respected as I deserve to be. I'm going to organize my house and the family's priorities, and I'm going to pursue my professional dream, in that order—respecting the priorities and building pillars so as not to invert values.

On Action: My first action will be to take care of my appearance on a daily basis. My mind and my physique. Because I never prioritized it in the past, I believed I never had the time for it. I was in the mindset of limiting suffering.

Action 1: Starting tomorrow, I'm going to start the day by taking care of myself. I'm going to take a shower, take care of my skin, change my clothes, put on some make-up, and fix my hair. I will look beautiful every day. I will also meditate and pray before my daily activities. Beginning next Monday, I'm going to start walking for thirty minutes each day, at least three days a week. I will also change my diet to something healthier. I am going to take time out in my week to have coffee with my friends to be able to socialize.

Action 2: After twenty-one days, when I feel more centered, less emotionally shaken, and when my self-esteem improves a little, I will talk to my husband about our relationship and the way he treats me. I will tell him how I feel and how I would like to be treated. I will share with him the things that make me feel disrespected, and I'll let him know what I expect from him going forward. I will ask what he expects from me as well. This is a priority I am not willing to compromise.

Action 3: Working on my family's priorities to move on to the step of starting to establish the fourth step, the professional one. I will start to take steps little by little toward my dream and conquests.

Mindfulness: Today, I deal wisely and responsibly with the demands of my home, my husband's personality, the demands of my children, and the difficulties and problems presented in my life and in my relationships. I will do this without losing myself. Because I decided to build in myself what I was expecting to receive from everyone around me. I wanted them to help me, listen to me, forgive me, and build me up. And that was not on them. Today, I know my worth, who I am, and where I'm going. Everyone respects me, and I have boundaries in my relationships. I found it all within myself, thanks to God and to this Freedom Technique that helped me live the newness that Jesus conquered for me.

Today, I'm a caregiver for the elderly, I help women build their self-love, I build this pattern of self-love within my work with them. My marriage is stable, and we have a good, respectful relationship. We're continually working on our relationship, but today, we respect each other's space. My kids have a stable house to call home, all thanks to God.

These were a couple examples of altered but real patients who were able to change situations around completely through the implementation of the Freedom Technique in therapy sessions with Michelle, and through consistent practice of it at home. It takes work. Remember, simple does not equal easy. But in the end, it's worth it.

These patients, as well as Michelle, give all the glory to God. He is the One who made it all possible, and He is the One who gave Michelle this incredible technique that she's now sharing with others.

In Closing

We're so happy that we were able to put into words a work that can now help so many. The Freedom Technique will help you in such practical ways, as God continues to unveil you to become fully alive, encounter your full potential and purpose, and live the freedom and victory that was purchased for you at the cross. You deserve it. Not because of anything you did, but because He chose it that way. He chose *you*. Now go live freely!

Credits—Freedom Technique

Credit to the Bible. The first structure of the technique gained shape mirrored in the steps of the tent of meeting created by Moses in the desert. The steps consisted of acts of worship to God, including the people admitting their sins as an act of responsibility. Through these steps, man would reach forgiveness of wrongdoings and actions. First, they would submit to sacrifice, because their sins and wrongdoings had pushed them away from the presence of God. In this place was the door, the burnt offering (place of sacrifice), the washbasin, the veils setting off another more separate area of the temple, the lampstand, the bread tray, the incense, and finally, the sacred place.

Credit to the psychoanalytic method for bringing out the repressed unconscious and strengthening the ego.

Credit to cognitive behavioral therapy (CBT) techniques for challenging limiting perceptions and revealing thoughts and feelings, and sharpening to see other angles and changing behaviors.

Credit to neuroscience for discovering the possibility of neuroplasticity in the brain.

Credit to epigenetics for studying how behaviors and environment can cause changes that affect the way genes work.

The End

BONUS

Empowering Identity Declarations

There's nothing more freeing and renewing than declaring the truth over ourselves about who we are. I suggest that you highlight the bullet points below in bright yellow, then go back to them daily. Read them and declare them over yourself as often as you would like, until it truly transforms you.

Feel free to add more bullet points, Bible verses, or simply a truth that you feel God speaking to you. The truth of the Word of God is absolutely transforming, and it will set you free.

- I am the salt of the earth (Matthew 5:13).
- I am the light of the world (Matthew 5:14).
- I am valuable to God (Matthew 6:26).
- I am indwelled by Christ; His Spirit lives in me (John 14:20).
- I am a branch of the true vine (John 15:15).
- I am Christ's friend (John 15:15).
- I am chosen and appointed by Christ to go and bear fruit (John 15:16).
- I am justified by the blood of Jesus Christ (Romans 5:9).
- I am reconciled to God through Christ's death and saved through Christ's life (Romans 5:10).
- I am set free from sin and have become a slave to righteousness (Romans 6:18).
- I am free from condemnation (Romans 8:1).
- I am a child of God and a co-heir with Christ (Romans 8:17).
- I am more than a conqueror through Christ (Romans 8:37).
- I am accepted by Christ (Romans 15:7).
- I am blessed and highly favored! I am fruitful, and I multiply

all that God puts in my hands! (Genesis 1:28; Ephesians 1:3).
- I am a new creature in Christ, and old things have passed away; I am not my mistakes—my mistakes do not define me (2 Corinthians 5:17).
- I am righteous in Christ (2 Corinthians 5:21).
- I am dead to sin and alive unto righteousness (Romans 6:11).
- I've been set free! I am free to love, to worship and to trust, with no fear of rejection or of being hurt (John 8:36; Romans 8:1).
- I am a believer, not a doubter (Mark 5:36).
- I am creative, because the Holy Spirit lives in me (John 14:26; 1 Corinthians 6:19).
- I am fully forgiven and free from all shame and condemnation (Romans 8:1-2; Ephesians 1:7-8; 1 John 1:19).
- I have no fear or anxiety; I trust the Lord with all my heart (Proverbs 3:5-6; Philippians 4:6-7; 1 Peter 5:7).
- I am fully able to fulfill the calling God has placed in my life (Exodus 3:9-12; Psalm 57:2; Colossians 1:24-29).
- My sins are forgiven; God doesn't remember them anymore, and neither will I; I am free from sin (Hebrews 8:12; 1 John 1:9).
- I am the bride of Christ (Revelation 21:9).
- The blood of Jesus Christ justifies me (Romans 5:9).
- I am a child of God, heir of God, chosen by God; I am holy, a saint, and dearly loved by Him! (1 John 3:1-2; Galatians 4:7; Ephesians 1:1, 1:11, 1:5; Colossians 3:12).
- I am responsible; I enjoy embracing responsibility and I rise up to every responsibility in Christ Jesus (2 Corinthians 11:28; Philippians 4:13).
- I forgive others as God has forgiven me (Luke 11:4).
- I have the mind of Christ (1 Corinthians 2:16).
- I am the temple of God; His Spirit lives in me (1 Corinthians 3:16, 6:19).
- I am washed, justified, and sanctified through Christ (1 Corinthians 6:11).
- I am an important part of the body of Christ (1 Corinthians 12:27).
- I am the fragrance of Christ (2 Corinthians 2:15).
- I am an ambassador of Christ and a minister of reconciliation

(2 Corinthians 5:20).
- I am redeemed from the curse of the law (Galatians 3:13).
- I am redeemed and forgiven through Christ's blood (Ephesians 1:7).
- I am now alive with Christ (Ephesians 2:5).
- I am God's workmanship, created in Christ Jesus to do good works, which God has prepared in advance for me to do (Ephesians 2:10).
- I am a fellow citizen with God's people and a member of God's household (Ephesians 2:19).
- I (as a woman) am a helper, and I am able (Genesis 2:18; Philippians 4:13).
- I am unique (Genesis 2:21).
- I am powerful, I am an enemy of the devil, I am born of God, and the evil one cannot harm me (Genesis 3:15; 1 John 5:18; 1 Peter 5:8).
- I am a citizen of heaven (Philippians 3:20).
- I am complete in Christ (Colossians 2:10).
- I am rescued from the dominion of darkness and brought into the kingdom of light (Colossians 1:13).
- I am hidden with Christ in God (Colossians 3:3).
- I am part of a chosen people, a royal priesthood, a holy nation, a people belonging to God, to declare the praises of Him who called us out of darkness into His wonderful light (1 Peter 2:9-10).
- I am an alien and a stranger in this world (1 Peter 2:11).
- I am FREE! (Romans 8:2).

BONUS

More Empowering Scriptures on Biblical Freedom

Here are more scriptures on my research of biblical freedom that I didn't include earlier. It's a lot, and not everyone is a big fan of this much research. But it's so good that I didn't want to leave it out—for those who love it as much as I do!

> "'At that time I will bring you in, yes, at the time I gather you together; for I will make you a name and a praise among all the peoples of the earth when I restore your fortunes [and freedom] before your eyes,' says the Lord." (Zephaniah 3:20 AMP)

Freedom is to be restored—restored back to the beginning, back to our original form and purpose.

> "Let no one defraud you of your prize [your freedom in Christ and your salvation] by insisting on mock humility and the worship of angels, going into detail about visions [he claims] he has seen [to justify his authority], puffed up [in conceit] by his unspiritual mind." (Colossians 2:18 AMP)

Freedom is our prize in Christ! Christ died for our freedom and salvation; the price has been paid. Freedom is our right as a child of God. Simple as that!

> "Look at the birds of the air; they neither sow [seed] nor reap [the harvest] nor gather [the crops] into barns, and yet

your heavenly Father keeps feeding them. Are you not worth much more than they?" (Matthew 6:26 AMP)

Freedom is to understand our worth and to believe that God will feed us in every way we may need to be fed. This means we aren't living our lives worried about everything.

> "Even though I am free of the demands and expectations of everyone, I have voluntarily become a servant to any and all in order to reach a wide range of people." (1 Corinthians 9:19 MSG)

Freedom is acting in selflessness. Being selfless has to be one of the truest demonstrations of freedom. We can be truly selfless only when we understand that we don't do it because we have to, but because we want to—for the sake of being good ambassadors of Christ.

> "Those who think they can do it on their own end up obsessed with measuring their own moral muscle but never get around to exercising it in real life. Those who trust God's action in them find that God's Spirit is in them—living and breathing God! Obsession with self in these matters is a dead end; attention to God leads us out into the open, into a spacious, free life. Focusing on the self is the opposite of focusing on God. Anyone completely absorbed in self ignores God, ends up thinking more about self than God. That person ignores who God is and what he is doing. And God isn't pleased at being ignored." (Romans 8:6-8 MSG)

Freedom is understanding, acting, and behaving according to our true nature in Christ, the nature of the Spirit, and not to give attention to our old nature or think that we still have it in us at all.

God and evil cannot coexist. If we have His nature—which, in fact, we do—and if we've accepted Jesus as our Lord and Savior, then we can no longer claim we have our old sinful nature. Nor can we behave as if we did. We must understand the One from whom our new nature comes, so we may allow our behaviors to follow Him.

"If the Son makes you free, then you are unquestionably free." (John 8:36 AMP)

Freedom is to accept everything Christ has paid for us to have. John 8:36 is one of my favorite verses on freedom. Just think: *If the Son has set you free, you are free indeed.* But we must accept what He has done for us. We must accept the freedom and understand what it truly is. And this is exactly what we did in this book. By now, I'm sure you have a whole new perspective on this verse!

"I was blameless before Him, and I kept myself free from my sin." (Psalm 18:23 AMP)

Freedom includes not being controlled by sin. Does this mean we will never sin? No, it doesn't mean that. We may sin and make a mistake. But if we do, we repent, go to Jesus, accept His forgiveness, and move on. We don't allow sin to condemn us, control us, take us over. We don't live by sin. If we sin, we aren't comfortable with that sin; we promptly repent and do not sin on purpose or repeatedly over and over. That's what it means to not be slaves of sin.

"The faith which you have [that gives you freedom of choice], have as your own conviction before God [just keep it between yourself and God, seeking His will]. Happy is he who has no reason to condemn himself for what he approves." (Romans 14:22 AMP)

Freedom is to have our will so aligned with the will of God and to grab hold of His righteousness so strongly that the devil has nothing that can be used to condemn us.

"Therefore, believers, since we have confidence and full freedom to enter the Holy Place [the place where God dwells] by [means of] the blood of Jesus." (Hebrews 10:19 AMP)

Freedom is to know that we have access to God anywhere and anytime! When Jesus shed His blood on the cross, He gave us access to the Holy of Holies, where we find God's presence, peace, and freedom. There's no place where we go to access that. It's inside each of us. Freedom is understanding that God has chosen to inhabit us, and accepting that the blood of Jesus was enough to make that a reality.

> "He expected his countrymen to understand that God was granting them freedom through him [assuming that they would accept him], but they did not understand." (Acts 7:25 AMP)

Freedom is to understand God's desire for humanity. We are free not because we deserve to be or even want to be. We are free because freedom is God's desire for humanity. We cannot be free without knowing the Freedom Giver.

Freedom is to have the light of God in every area of our lives:

> "The LORD is God, and He has given us light [illuminating us with His grace and freedom and joy]. Bind the festival sacrifices with cords to the horns of the altar." (Psalm 118:27 AMP)

The enemy often makes us think that some things are better off kept in darkness. He whispers in our ears, "If people knew that about you, they wouldn't like you, they would think less of you, so don't say anything."

That's a lie from the pit of hell. The enemy keeps it there and uses it to shame us, blame us, and steal our joy. And it keeps us from experiencing God's freedom in that area. By shedding the light of God in every area and every situation, we're set free from all negative emotions that the secret in the darkness brought upon us. Freedom is the absence of darkness in every area of our lives.

> "The Spirit of the Lord GOD is upon me,
> because the LORD has anointed and commissioned me
> to bring good news to the humble and afflicted;
> He has sent me to bind up [the wounds of] the brokenhearted,
> to proclaim release [from confinement and condemnation] to the [physical and spiritual] captives
> and freedom to prisoners." (Isaiah 61:1 AMP)

Freedom is both physical and spiritual. Freedom is transferable from one spirit to another through the power of the Holy Spirit in us, the anointing of God in our lives, and the authority given to believers by Jesus Christ, the Anointed One. There's more to freedom than just physical freedom or the absence of chains holding someone captive. There is mental, emotional, and spiritual freedom.

> "It is absolutely clear that God has called you to a free life. Just make sure that you don't use this freedom as an excuse to do whatever you want to do and destroy your freedom. Rather, use your freedom to serve one another in love; that's how freedom grows. For everything we know about God's Word is summed up in a single sentence: Love others as you love yourself. That's an act of true freedom. If you bite and ravage each other, watch out—in no time at all you will be annihilating each other, and where will your precious freedom be then?" (Galatians 5:13-15 MSG)

Freedom is given to us to serve and seek the best for one another in love. Freedom allows us to live for others with the assurance that Jesus lives for us. We grow and become a better reflection of Him every day.

Freedom is also to serve without expecting anything in return, without the need for earthly recognition, and with an unselfish motive and heart.

> "For my part, I am going to boast about nothing but the Cross of our Master, Jesus Christ. Because of that Cross, I have been crucified in relation to the world, set free from the stifling atmosphere of pleasing others and fitting into the little patterns that they dictate. Can't you see the central issue in all this? It is not what you and I do—submit to circumcision, reject circumcision. It is what God is doing, and he is creating something totally new, a free life! All who walk by this standard are the true Israel of God—his chosen people. Peace and mercy on them!" (Galatians 6:14-15 MSG)

Freedom is to understand and truly embrace our new nature

in Christ. I can't say this enough! If God repeated it over and over throughout the Bible, it must be important, right? Understand that whatever used to enslave us must no longer do so. We're empowered to walk away from whatever doesn't belong to our lives in Christ. This is so powerful and so freeing!

I hope you enjoyed the couple extra chapters I included here for you!

About the Author

Tassyane Assis is an ordained minister and teacher of the Word of God, helping many to be set free from imprisoning mindsets and to walk in freedom and restoration. Her educational background and degrees are in business administration and biblical and hermeneutical studies. Tassyane completed multiple writing, publishing, and author development courses, mentorships, and coaching programs, and has acquired a book publisher certificate from IAP Career College. She is also a certified life coach and has helped many to grow spiritually and emotionally by overcoming wrong belief systems and replacing them with biblical truth. In the business world, she has been leading and coaching both individuals and groups for over two decades, and has helped many achieve their goals and aspirations.

Tassyane loves people deeply and fiercely. Her personal life mission is to partner with God to help translate God's unseen realm and heart to believers, to teach the truth with simplicity, and to help transform individuals through divine revelations that will lead them into encounters with Jesus that bring restoration and freedom. She believes that everything we do flows from who we are in Christ, and from a deep and intimate relationship with Him.

Tassyane has been writing since childhood, and she believes it to be an expression of not only her own heart and creativity, but also of the Holy Spirit in and through her. She has written numerous Bible studies and continues to do so. Some of them can be found on her blog at tassyaneassis.com.

Tassyane was born and raised in Brazil and moved to America as a teenager with her mother and two of her younger siblings. She's the oldest of eight children. (Her dad took seriously God's command to multiply!) Today, she resides in the beautiful sunshine of South

Florida with her husband, three grown children, and their dog.

She would love to connect with you on social media—@tassyane.assis. You can also visit her website to connect as well, where she posts weekly thoughts about freedom, love, and life in general, and your thoughts are appreciated.

Made in the USA
Coppell, TX
03 January 2024